Christian
Teachers
— in —
Public
Schools

A Guide for Teachers, Administrators, and Parents

Christian Teachers —in— Public Schools

Julia K. Stronks and Gloria Goris Stronks

Baker Books
A Division of Baker Book House Co
Grand Rapids, Michigan 49516

Published by Baker Books
a division of Baker Book House Company
P.O. Box 6287, Grand Rapids, MI 49516-6287

Printed in the United States of America

Library of Congress Cataloging-in-Publication Data

Stronks, Julia K.
    Christian teachers in public schools : a guide for teachers, administrators, and parents / Julia K. Stronks and Gloria Goris Stronks.
        p.   cm.
    Includes bibliographical references.
    ISBN 0-8010-5844-9 (pbk.)
    1. Religion in the public schools—United States. 2. Christian teachers—United States. 3. Christian teachers—United States—Interviews. 4. Teaching—Religious aspects—Christianity. 5. Religious education—Law and legislation—United States. I. Stronks, Gloria Goris. II. Title.
LC111.S737 1999
379.2'8'0973—dc21   98-43520

For information about academic books, resources for Christian leaders, and all new releases available from Baker Book House, visit our web site:
http://www.bakerbooks.com

Contents

98498

Preface

We wrote this book for Christian teachers who have followed their calling to teach in state-supported or public schools. Aware that their task is of great importance, many of these teachers struggle to obey the law while trying to teach in ways that are authentic to their personal beliefs. Other teachers believe morals and values are in such need at this time that teaching them should take priority over the law. We hope this book will open discussion among Christian teachers and provide some answers. Although we both are presently teaching in Christian colleges, one of us is also an attorney and has taught in a state university. The other has spent many years teaching in public and Christian schools.

Christian Teachers in Public Schools begins with an explanation of the tensions Christians may feel when they teach in public schools. These tensions arise from their own desire to teach with integrity, the expectations parents have concerning their children's education, and both parties' understanding of what the law does and does not allow. Chapter 2 explains why Christian teachers may teach from a perspective that reflects their beliefs while at the same time not advocating for those beliefs. In chapter 3 we describe how teachers may plan curriculum and instruction that are true to their Christian beliefs while still obeying the law.

The second half of the book, chapters 4, 5, and 6, examines the legal rights and responsibilities of Christian teachers in public school classrooms. Chapter 4 clarifies the intent of the religion clauses of the First Amendment to the U.S. Constitution and explains the significance of two federal laws designed to protect religious voices in the public arena. Chapter 5 uses a question-and-answer format to address common concerns of the public school teacher along with ways in which teachers and school districts can reduce the threat of litigation. Chapter 6 explains the argument Christians have with those who say public schools are religion-free, and it explains why some Christians say education cannot be neutral toward religion. While these chapters address developments in U.S. constitutional law, there are parallels between U.S. law and the laws of England, Canada, and Australia. We hope these chapters will encourage Christian teachers in all nations to think about what the law in their country allows.

The final chapter contains conversations with Christian teachers concerning how they are following their call to teach in public schools.

The quotations from teachers that appear throughout the book, including those in the final chapter, have been taken from our written surveys and oral interviews. While we thought it would be wise to change teachers' names in the body of the book to protect their schools and their positions in those schools, the names of many teachers who participated in the surveys and interviews are listed here: Kenneth L. Andree, Mel Andree, Melissa Austin, Joy L. Baird, Lynnell Berkompas, Grace Post Bradford, Jacqueline Decker, Carol Den Otter, Lydia Ann Foley, Jim Gilford, Christine K. Grailier,

Janice Hollander, Jonathan Holthaus, Susan Hornor, Gail Hosmer, Coni Huisman, Nella Johnson, Lynn Klamer Morrow, Joe Kliefisch, John Knox, Norma Knox, Laura Kopenski, Karen Kuck, Margaret Lanning, Melissa Lantinga, Colleen Lokers, John Magnuson, Sharon Mast, Randy Mickelsen, Judi Migliazzo, Evelyn Mohr, Brenda Mulroy, Jim Poll, Martin Reitsma, Ruth Ryskamp, Amy Scheuermann, Dan Swadley, David Taylor, Carolyn Thacker, Arne Vroom, Judy Vroom, Gary Vruggink, Joyce Walkes, Daniel Ward, Aukje Wonnacott, Don Wonnacott, and Marilyn Zondervan. Many additional interviewees asked that they not be acknowledged. We are enormously grateful to these teachers who so willingly gave their time to participate in the surveys and interviews. Without their help the project could not have been completed.

We are grateful to Whitworth College and Calvin College for the time they have made available to us to work on this project. The Calvin College Alumni Association provided a grant to cover the cost of interviewing teachers in different parts of North America. Our student assistants, Jennifer Knox De Jong, Amy Den Otter, Tammy Milne Wiersma, and Laura Walker, provided invaluable help with researching documents and conducting interviews. Teacher education students who plan to teach in public schools read and critiqued drafts of chapters. Our colleagues engaged in teacher education at Calvin College and at The Institute for Christian Studies and Redeemer College, both in Ontario, Canada, were not only helpful but most encouraging. We are especially grateful to the following Christian college faculty members who contributed their reflections on ways their faith shaped their instruction while teaching at secular universities: Rick Faber (Dordt College), Jim Jadritch (Calvin College), Diana Trotter (Whitworth College), and Sheri Lantinga (Dordt College). We also would like to thank Robert Hosack and Melinda Van Engen for their enthusiastic support and helpful suggestions.

Both of us have had to work through our own responses to the question: How can I teach in a public school or university in a way that is true to my Christian commitment? We have learned a great deal from others while writing this book, but most of all we have come to appreciate the cloud of witnesses that surrounds the children and young people in our nations' schools.

1 Walking a Fine Line

The teacher stood at the window of her seventh-grade classroom watching the students line up for the first day of school. She already knew many of them because she had seen them around school last year. There was Vernon with his sandy hair and dusting of freckles across his nose; Randy with his black eyes darting around, waiting for something funny to happen; Jennie standing, as usual, off by herself until the last bell rang. Two boys she hadn't seen before had just returned from a residence for delinquent children. What would she be able to do for and with all of them during the coming year? Of course she would strive to be caring, thoughtful, and fair and would work hard to help them learn. She knew it would be wrong to be directly evangelistic with them, but was showing fairness and loving concern all she could do?

It takes courage to be a Christian teacher in a public school. Leaders in Christian and secular communities alike have severely criticized public schools for poor behavior of students, inappropriate selection of textbooks, and teachers who are too uninformed, lazy, or unwilling to teach a rigorous curriculum. While there surely are reasons for criticism of some schools, teachers everywhere hear those words as rebuke for the work they are doing under difficult circumstances. Teachers who are attempting to fulfill their Christian calling within legal guidelines feel an even greater frustration.

When we refer to "public schools" in this book, we mean those schools that are supported by the state for the purpose of educating students of every race and ability. Within the United States the term is easily understood, but in countries such as The Netherlands and Australia, along with some Canadian provinces, a great variety of schools receive federal or provincial funding. In those cases, the phrase "public schools" usually refers to the schools that are not associated with a particular worldview or religious perspective. An excellent description of the different types of schools and the complexity of the task that faces public schools in a pluralistic democracy can be found in Charles Glenn's *The Myth of the Common School* (1988).

Children and adolescents who attend school today have very different lives than those who lived even two generations earlier. There was a time in North American schools when a teacher could raise children's expectations of the life they would someday live—a life open to marvelous possibilities. A child born into that world was encouraged to make active choices that would influence the person he or she would someday become. Teachers said, "You can become anything you choose to become," and told students stories of famous people who had succeeded in spite of great difficulties.

Today that world of wonderful possibilities is only a partial truth. The gap between those who have the background to follow their dreams and those who hardly dare dream at all is enormous and growing wider every day. We speak about children living "below the poverty level," but that phrase does not even begin to describe the abject misery in which some children live. For many children, home is even more dreadful than a place where food and shelter are inadequate. For them, home is an unsafe place filled with misery. Such children hardly know how to survive, much less to dream. In other cases, children grow up in safe homes in which they are free to dream, but they are encouraged to dream in ways that are individualistic and self-centered. They see around them adults who believe that their own wishes and desires are of primary importance and that success can be achieved by learning to manipulate people and events to make outcomes conform to their wishes. Peter Kreeft (1992) suggests that we are living in a time in which self-control is lacking in many people's lives as they pursue their own desires. Children and adults who cannot control themselves are at the mercy of outside forces. This is particularly dangerous at a time when television, videos, and the Internet have brought violence and many other kinds of inappropriate and disruptive behavior into their homes.

It is still true, however, as Max van Manen (1991) suggests, that children must believe in the possibility of success if they are to become educated:

> The modern child must actively realize that he or she is born into a condition of possibilities. He or she *is* this body of possibilities. To become a person, to grow up and to become educated, is to transform one's contingency into commitment responsibility—one must choose a life. (p. 3)

Van Manen goes on to say that teachers are the ones who can shape these life choices. That may sound marvelously optimistic to teachers faced with the day-to-day task of surviving each day's fearful challenges. Yet, if teachers cannot work toward helping children and adolescents to choose a worthwhile life that is valuable to themselves and to others, there is often no one else left to do so. Many children and adolescents do not have the kind of parental support and guidance they need, and often teachers are the only ones left to fill this gap. This means that teachers are the only ones who will help these students learn to recognize the dangers of drug use and how to deal with the violence that is a part of daily life in and around some schools. For many students, teachers are the only adults who will help them make wise decisions concerning their sexuality. Unfortunately, the task of shaping lives in today's world has become increasingly difficult to the point at which even Christian teachers despair and wonder whether what they are doing or saying has any effect at all on students.

The Concerns of Christian Teachers

Are Christian teachers capable of providing the direction needed to fill the gap left in the lives of many students? In preparation for this book, we conducted interviews with public school teachers throughout the United States and parts of Canada and discovered that many long-term teachers speak privately of their understanding that each student is made in the image of God. Yet, when the same teachers were asked whether they feel called to teach in a public school, their answers suggested that they do recognize the call but that the activities of the school day often interfere with all that responding to such a call implies. It is easy to lose track of one's purpose in school when one is caught up in the daily business and busyness of getting the system to work as well as it should. Still, one has to recognize the implications of the call if one is to engage in the struggle.

James Schwartz (1997) describes three distinct roles Christian teachers see for themselves as they struggle to fulfill their calling.

1. *Agent for Enculturation.* These teachers believe God has called them to be an influence for good in the lives of

school children. They can only fulfill this purpose, however, if they retain the goodwill of the school community. As a result, they steer clear of any controversial roles or the expression of personal points of view concerning religion to avoid jeopardizing that goodwill.

2. *Christian Advocate/Evangelist.* These teachers believe they must act as "undercover agents" or infiltrators seeking ways to provide a Christian perspective on the things they teach, even if they must take risks and test the limits of church-state separation.

3. *Golden Rule Truth-Seeker.* A teacher who sees himself or herself in this role would introduce worldview questions into the study of culture with the purpose of identifying and responding justly to the source of differences among people in a pluralistic society.

In social studies or literature classes this teacher might ask questions such as:

What kind of war might be considered a war that is fought for just reasons?
What might a perfect community look like? How would people in that community ensure that all citizens would be treated justly? Would there be poverty in such a community and, if so, what would be done to help those who live in poverty?
What does it mean to be a person of honor?

In science or math classes this teacher might ask:

Should we use artificial means to keep people alive as long as possible?
Is it appropriate to spend money on a space program when there is so much poverty in the world?
To what extent does the use of technology change us? Does it ever get in the way of relationships?

> How would you respond to a person who, like the Amish, says that before we use any new technology we should ask ourselves, "How will the introduction of this new technology change us?"
>
> What is infinity? The philosopher Descartes likened the concept of infinity to God. What do you think about that?

The Golden Rule Truth-Seeker would have a somewhat less abrasive view of her role than would the Christian Advocate/Evangelist. At the same time, the Golden Rule Truth-Seeker would agree with the Christian Advocate/Evangelist that the Agent for Enculturation is too accommodating of secularism. Instead of keeping the religious questions largely private, as the Agent for Enculturation would do, the Golden Rule Truth-Seeker would attempt to treat religious questions and concerns as a normal and healthy part of public human life. (p. 295)

Schwartz admits it is unlikely that a teacher would neatly fit into just one of these positions. It is more likely that he or she would function in one role at one particular time and in another role at another time. Although he appreciates the value in each of the roles, he believes the position of Golden Rule Truth-Seeker offers the best model for Christian teachers in the public school. He reasons that the Golden Rule Truth-Seeker role encourages teachers to explore with their students their religious liberty, consider philosophical and religious questions in a structured program, and pose worldview questions in the study of various parts of the curriculum.

Schwartz's categories are helpful to experienced teachers as they think about ways to integrate their faith into their professional lives. These descriptions would also be of help to many beginning teachers who, in spite of having graduated from Christian colleges, often concentrate so carefully on classroom climate, lesson preparation, and getting to know their students that they give little thought to what it might mean to "teach Christianly" (Hill, 1982). Recognizing the difficulty of doing so is what makes education majors uneasy about teaching in the public school. Of course a Christian teacher must strive to be caring, thoughtful, and fair with students and work hard to help them grow in the right direction. Of course it is wrong to be directly evangelistic with students in the classroom. But is showing fairness and loving concern all one can do? Our interviews show that beginning teachers in public school settings were often puzzled when they were asked what teaching Christianly means to them, and they questioned whether it is possible or legitimate to do so in their school.

While it is true that some teachers lack the understanding necessary to struggle with the issue of being called to teach in a public school, others admit they also lack the courage to address the issue and to find an appropriate response. The call to teach is a call to be with others, and yet it is, paradoxically, a lonely calling. Many Christian teachers say that at times they feel a loneliness that cannot be described—a depletion. Ann put it this way:

Early in my teaching career I was teaching in a school close to the downtown area of a large city. Many of my fifth graders were troubled children who needed close watching, and so when the motorcade of the president of the United States was scheduled to pass just a block from the school, the principal decided it would be better if we watched it on television rather than in person. We had just studied the civil rights movement, and the Kennedy assassination was fresh in our minds. Suddenly I realized that Marvin, a very troubled student, was muttering something under his breath. I stepped closer and heard him whisper over and over, "I hate that man. I'm gonna kill that man if I get a chance." I moved my chair so I could sit beside Marvin and put my hand on his trembling arm, and eventually the whispering and shaking stopped. Months of teaching students who were so needy left me exhausted and lonely, wondering where there was help for them . . . or for me.

It is possible that Christian teachers in public schools experience discouragement and burnout because they have not understood the importance of developing a way of thinking that will allow their world-and-life view to guide their teaching. Therefore, they encounter uneasy moments when they wonder whether they could have done more in a given situation. To teach without a framework within which one can make decisions means that each new decision must be rethought—an exhausting business, to say the least.

Kathleen Norris, in *The Cloister Walk,* tells of a desert monastic of fourth-century Egypt who said, "It is impossible for us to be surrounded by worldly honor and at the same time to bear heavenly fruit" (p. 76). There are few places in which one is likely to get so little worldly honor as when teaching in a public school, but there are also few places in which heavenly fruit is so much needed.

Many teachers say they would like to talk about their faith with other teachers, but for some reason they rarely engage in conversations about what it is to teach Christianly in a state-supported school. They admit they are often disturbed at the ease with which different learning theories subtly direct classroom management and shape the learning environment, and they desire the support of other Christians who struggle with these issues. Because that support is not present, many cease to wrestle to align their educational practice with their Christian commitment. They are also often uncertain about what state and constitutional laws allow them to say and do in a public school and, as a result, do all they can to avoid giving offense.

A public school superintendent addressed this issue in an interview:

> You asked whether, during my tenure as superintendent, there have been many court cases concerning teachers who have caused offense by being too open about their Christian faith in the classroom. I don't recall ever having had that

issue arise in all of my years of experience. In fact, in my opinion, the opposite has been true. Many Christian teachers have bent over backwards to avoid stepping over the line, and the students have not had the benefit of knowing their teachers as people of deep religious faith. Of course, the law must be obeyed. However, in a time when students so much need direction in knowing what is right or wrong, we need teachers who can provide that direction.

In addition, in communities in which Christian schools exist, many public school teachers have chosen to be silent about their work because, whether or not it is true, they fear there is an underlying judgment concerning their choice of service in the kingdom. They wonder whether it is true, as some argue, that teaching from a Christian perspective can only occur in a Christian school. They bristle under the implication that they have chosen to teach in a public school because the salaries are higher than those in Christian schools. Jane, the spouse of a public school teacher, put it this way:

I have always felt pressure, even from family members, that Monty should have been teaching in Christian schools. They asked if it was for the money. It wasn't until the last ten years that our pastors even prayed for Christian teachers in public schools. Of course our pastor has three council members who teach in public schools. That likely makes a difference. And often families in the church who send their children to the public school feel much more rapport with Monty [because he is there]. They can appreciate what he is doing. They can't afford to send their children to the Christian school, and they think it is wonderful to have Christian teachers in the school.

Christian teachers are not alone in their work even on the days when, after the last bell, they feel only relief and despair. If they truly believe they were brought into their students' lives so that they will be there for each student and will pray for them, God will not allow these teachers to founder but will support them as they live out their calling. Ann stated:

> In my first years of teaching in public schools, there were many things I didn't understand that I do understand now. Perhaps the most important was that during my prayer time at home I needed to pray individually for my students. Oh, I always prayed that I would be a good teacher for them and that we would work well together as God wanted us to. But I didn't, at that time, understand that perhaps God wanted me in those students' lives because I was likely the only one who would ever bring each of those names before the throne of grace. I truly regret the years I taught without understanding that.

Lori added:

> I think the biggest way my faith has influenced my relationship with the children I have taught has been to recognize each child's uniqueness. I have taught in two school systems that were at each end of the spectrum. The first school was in a small rural community . . . where the parents were almost all on welfare. The second school system was in an affluent area. Where all the children in my previous school were in the free lunch program, no child in my second school received even reduced-priced lunches. Though these children in both schools contrasted so much, I always prayed for each child and his or her future, as well as for guidance as to how best to meet the needs of each one.

The difficulty comes, of course, when teachers find themselves longing for their classroom and school to be a true community but seeing them fall far short of that goal. They remember how school was when they were children, and they grieve for a time and place that are no more. Moreover, there is a longing for God's shalom in a place in which teachers fear it will never happen. Still, teachers who pray individually for children often find that their personal walk with them is transformed. They know that the God who can turn "the desert into pools of water and the parched ground into flowing springs" (Ps. 107:35) can also change relationships in a classroom. Along the way, teachers will be helped a great deal if they can share the burden and blessing of their work with other teachers who are like-minded.

The Concerns of Christian Parents

It is no secret that there is tension between some Christian parents and the public schools their children attend. One cause of this tension is confusion on the part of the parents over what is occurring in their child's development. For example, at the middle-school level the intellectual, emotional, and physical development of students varies considerably and teachers work hard to create a learning environment appropriate to those changes. Alex Molnar (1994) says, however, that parents who are concerned about their child becoming a "moody, self-absorbed, rebellious stranger" often think it is the middle school's fault.

> Behaviors that educators regarded as predictable during the turbulent transition of adolescence, parents might think of as precipitated by whatever it was their child was doing in middle school. I could imagine a mother or father remembering the summer before middle school when a happy, loving child eagerly took part in family activities. Then, suddenly, apparently for no other reason than moving from elementary to middle school, he or she turned into some sort of monster. What were they doing in that middle school anyway? . . . Part of the job of public school educators is explaining the logic behind the school curriculum to community members, soliciting their ideas, and being willing to participate with them in defining and directing the school program. (p. 5)

Molnar goes on to suggest that educators should explain to parents the changes they can expect in their child before those changes occur. The concerns that Christian parents express often reflect their lack of awareness; they are not prepared for the normal developmental changes their child will go through. When the changes cause disturbance in the family, the parents wonder if the school is the source of the problem.

Another cause for confusion is that there is no one set of beliefs concerning education in public schools to which all Christians adhere. Some Christian parents want their children to have a great deal of freedom to think in new ways as they develop, believing that children must learn to become all that God has made it possible for them to be. Other Christian parents want their children to have very little freedom and expect the school to be restrictive and to "train" them in ways that will keep them free from trouble. Then there are Christian parents who believe that schools have no right to do more than inculcate basic skills. Christian parents who are delighted to discover that their child's teacher is a devout Christian can become extremely disappointed when that teacher's view of schooling is different from their own.

Christian parents have also expressed concern about the lack of neutrality in textbooks. They would like to protect their children from literature that refers to sexual activity or that is considered "vulgar" in any way. Some parent groups believe worldviews such as secular humanism or New Age religion are being taught through the textbooks used in public schools. In an article in *Educational Leadership,* Robert Marzano (1994) describes the attack by Christian fundamentalists on his widely used program *Tactics for Thinking.* Christian fundamentalist parents were convinced that in writing this program Marzano was part of a conspiracy to enlist children into an anti-Christian New Age religion. Marzano, a Roman Catholic, relates his understanding of ways in which his belief about the sinfulness of human nature led him into a far different operating principle from that used by those he calls "ultra fundamentalists." He suggests that parents and teachers keep an open dialogue concerning ways in which they may learn to communicate when their unprovable worldviews collide.

Teachers in many schools, confused by accusations that they are using materials that are part of the New Age movement, have said that their school offers a "secular program of study" consistent with the First Amendment prohibition of state-sponsored religion. Unfortunately, they have equated the absence of religion in the curriculum with constitutional neutrality in matters of faith. The Equal Access Act (1984), found constitutional by the Supreme Court, was passed to end "perceived widespread discrimination" against religious speech in public schools. Congress recognized the constitutional restrictions concerning government promotion of religion but said that non-school-sponsored student speech, including religious speech, should not be excised from the school environment. However, many teachers remain unclear as to whether student groups may meet to explore issues unrelated to the curriculum and whether outsiders who are neither students nor teachers may attend.

Christian parents have also become increasingly dissatisfied with a system of education that denies knowledge about religions to students. For example, Nicholas Piediscalzi, Paul Will, and Barbara Swyhart (1981) suggest that many who argue against prayer and Bible reading in public schools ignore the fact that the Supreme Court encouraged schools to teach about religions. The question is how should religion be taught in the public school?

Charles Haynes, in *Finding Common Ground: A First Amendment Guide to Religion and Public Education* (Haynes & Thomas, 1996), has provided a very helpful explanation of the difference between "teaching religion," which the Constitution does not allow, and "teaching about religions," which is allowed. Haynes's book describes ways in which knowledge of religions might be taught and provides resources for teaching about different world religions. If the public school is not to be a "religion-free zone," to use President Clinton's words, a copy of this book should have a place in the professional library of every public school.

Haynes (Haynes & Thomas, 1996) found general agreement among teachers, parents, and administrators that while public schools must protect the freedom of conscience of every student and parent, a quality education must include an understanding of the religious influences that have played a vital role in the molding of our nation. Haynes says that omission of instruction and discussion about religious and philosophical points of view in history, literature, and other subjects will give students the false impression that religious traditions and ways of believing are of only marginal importance in people's lives and that only nonreligious points of view are worthwhile (p. 1.3). If students are to learn to treat others with dignity and respect in increasingly diverse communities, they will need to understand ways of thinking that are different from their own. It is important that children and young people come to understand the religion of Muslims, Hindus, Buddhists, Christians, and Jews, among others, but many teachers are unclear concerning how that instruction is to take place.

This is especially true when teachers are faced with the argument that any attempt to teach children to respect another faith as much as their own is impossible; it will demean both faiths and cater to relativism. Charles and Joshua Glenn, in their interesting essay "Making Room for Religious Conviction in Democracy's Schools" (1992), quote a Muslim as saying:

> We should not adopt the ingenuous Western attitude that rites, traditions, and structures don't matter. They do matter, because they make us different, and they respect the val-

ues we hold dear; they should not be lightly shared, cheapened or trivialized in an attempt to promote multicultural understanding. That kind of understanding only begins with mutual respect. (In C. Glenn & J. Glenn, 1992, p. 108)

Concern for a pluralism that protects religious liberty prompted over one hundred political, religious, and educational leaders to craft The Williamsburg Charter (The Brookings Institution, 1990). This charter was framed to address the dilemmas, challenges, and opportunities posed by religious liberty in public life today. It calls for a reaffirmation of the principles that underlie religious liberty in America, a reappraisal of the course and conduct of recent public controversies, and a call for a reappropriating of the Constitution framers' vision and ideals in our time. It would help teachers to know of the curriculum materials that grew out of the charter, such as *Living with Our Deepest Differences: Religious Liberty in a Pluralistic Society* (Cassity, et. al., 1990) available for the upper elementary school.

Discussions about the way in which personal beliefs about life and about people color what we do and how we teach are important to our democratic society. But Haynes (Haynes & Thomas, 1996) warns that if discussions about the place of religion and values in school are to reflect the truest meanings of the First Amendment, they must take place with respect for each other and for the different views that are present.

Many people lament the loss of shared values and moral convictions that were part of their own public school education. Others say that instruction in such values can no longer take place in school because such diversity exists in our underlying beliefs. The next chapter will discuss the principles on which we may base the teaching of morals and values while still honoring our deepest differences.

②Teaching Morals and Values

Americans like to think of themselves as free, responsible people, and so when things go wrong, they look for some responsible person or institution to blame. Today, when people see problems in society, some tend to blame the public school system. Others blame families for their failure to raise children in a morally healthy way. For many people, therefore, the solution to societal ills is to be found in public school reform, starting with the teaching of character, values, and moral development. This call seems reasonable in light of the fact that failure to raise children with concern for moral development puts both children and society at risk. The problem, however, is that in our pluralistic society a consensus about what moral development means does not exist.

Christians fall into at least three camps over the issue of using Christianity to influence the moral development of all children in the public schools. Some believe that while faith should be protected privately, public institutions should not be used as tools to evangelize or to bring children to Christ. So, they might say, teach "faith neutral" morals. In other words, teach the morals and values that all people agree on, but leave Christianity out of it. Others believe that Christians should use every possible means to evangelize, and that if the mood of a community or the nation allows prayer in school, Christians should take advantage of it to promote their perspective. A third camp believes that although all of creation belongs to God and that Christians should reflect God's precepts in all areas of life, the Christian voice is one voice among many in the public square. Teachers in the public school, which is an arm of the government that must provide justice for all people, must recognize that this society is made up of people with competing views about truth. Christian teachers in the public school, therefore, should not use their positions to evangelize. This does not mean, however, that biblical truth is irrelevant or that it cannot be integrated into curriculum.

The Role of the State in the Morality Debate

When arguments about teaching morals in schools erupt, all sides act as imperialists (Marsden, 1997). The "diversity" advocates want everyone to think like they do, the conservative advocates want everyone to think like they do, and, all too often, the Christians want everyone to think like they do, ignoring the fact that even within Christianity there are many perspectives as to what it means to teach moral development. When any one group tries to determine moral values for the whole, the playing field becomes a battleground and children lose out.

Charles Haynes states that a central question for our world and for our schools is this: How will we live with our deepest differences?

Nowhere is the need to address this question greater than in public education. Not only are schools the storm center of controversy involving religious differences, they are the principal institution charged with transmitting the identity and mission of the United States from one generation to the next. If we fail in our school policies and classrooms to model and to teach how to live with differences, we endanger our experiment in religious liberty and our unity as a nation. (Haynes & Thomas, 1996, p. 1.2)

Haynes argues that we need to develop, out of our differences, a "common vision for the common good." Focusing on this vision can help us in determining how to look at the issue of teaching morals and values in schools. If we recognize that "rights are best guarded and responsibilities best exercised when each person and group guards for all others those rights they wish guarded for themselves," we will move toward a community that teaches children not only what to debate, but how to debate (Haynes & Thomas, 1996, p. 2.5). The following statement of principles was developed to guide civil discussion of conflicts in public schools.

Religious Liberty, Public Education, and the Future of American Democracy: A Statement of Principles

Our nation urgently needs a reaffirmation of our shared commitment, as American citizens, to the guiding principles of the Religious Liberty clauses of the First Amendment to the Constitution. The rights and responsibilities of the Religious Liberty clauses provide the civic framework within which we are able to debate our differences, to understand one another, and to forge public policies that serve the common good in public education.

Today, many American communities are divided over educational philosophy, school reform, and the role of religion and values in our public schools. Conflict and debate are vital to democracy. Yet, if controversies about public education are to advance the best interests of the nation, then how we debate, and not only what we debate, is critical.

In the spirit of the First Amendment, we propose the following principles as civic ground rules for addressing conflicts in public education.

Religious Liberty for All
Religious liberty is an inalienable right of every person. As Americans, we all share the responsibility to guard that right for every citizen. The Constitution of the United States with its Bill of Rights provides a civic framework of rights and responsibilities that enables Americans to work together for the common good in public education.

The Meaning of Citizenship
Citizenship in a diverse society means living with our deepest differences and committing ourselves to work for public policies that are in the best interest of all individuals, families, communities, and our nation. The framers of our Constitution referred to this concept of moral responsibility as civic virtue.

Public Schools Belong to All Citizens
Public schools must model the democratic process and constitutional principles in the development of policies and curricula. Policy decisions by officials or governing bodies should be made only after appropriate involvement of those affected by the decision and with due consideration for the rights of those holding dissenting views.

Religious Liberty and Public Schools
Public schools may not inculcate nor inhibit religion. They must be places where religion and religious conviction are treated with fairness and respect. Public schools uphold the First Amendment when they protect the religious liberty rights of students of all faiths or none. Schools demonstrate fairness when they ensure that the curriculum includes study about religion, where appropriate, as an important part of a complete education.

The Relationship between Parents and Schools
Parents are recognized as having the primary responsibility for the upbringing of their children, including education. Parents who send their children to public schools delegate to

public school educators some of the responsibility for their children's education. In so doing, parents acknowledge the crucial role of educators without abdicating their parental duty. Parents may also choose not to send their children to public schools and have their children educated at home or in private schools. However, private citizens, including business leaders and others, also have the right to expect public education to give students tools for living in a productive democratic society. All citizens must have a shared commitment to offer students the best possible education. Parents have a special responsibility to participate in the activity of their children's schools. Children and schools benefit greatly when parents and educators work closely together to shape school policies and practices and to ensure that public education supports the societal values of their community without undermining family values and convictions.

Conduct of Public Disputes

Civil debate, the cornerstone of a true democracy, is vital to the success of any effort to improve and reform America's public schools. Personal attacks, name-calling, ridicule, and similar tactics destroy the fabric of our society and undermine the educational mission of our schools. Even when our differences are deep, all parties engaged in public disputes should treat one another with civility and respect, and should strive to be accurate and fair. Through constructive dialogue we have much to learn from one another. (Haynes & Thomas, 1996, p. 2.2–2.3)

This statement is sponsored by twenty-one leading education organizations and religious groups. But is this discussion of pluralism really too much of a compromise? Shouldn't Christians work to claim the public school for Christ? Some Christians say that acceptance of the fact that people have different faith commitments leads to moral relativism. They argue that Christians should not give up their stand in claiming the one truth. Christian historian George Marsden of the University of Notre Dame states, however, that in a pluralistic society we have "little choice but to accept pragmatic standards in public life" (Marsden, 1997, p. 46). It is important to recognize, he says, that this does not necessarily put us on the road to relativism. Relativism occurs when liberal pragmatism is seen as an end in itself—when we think that the ultimate civic value is that which promotes civic discourse. This approach waters down beliefs into a "common faith," and it has no room for faiths that claim an ultimate truth to the exclusion of others. Instead, says Marsden, we should see liberal pragmatism not as an absolute good but as a legitimate method for dealing "peacefully and with equity among diverse peoples" (Marsden, 1997, p. 46). There is a difference between accepting a watered down "common faith" and developing a system that leads to the "common good." According to Marsden, our goal for the common good should be simple equity—emphasizing a fair balance for all voices at a time when cultural values are debated.

Christian philosopher Nicholas Wolterstorff explains that Christians can reject the Liberal/Enlightenment assumption that there is a religiously neutral common reason accessible to all but still work within the construct of liberal democracy in which all voices are encouraged to be part of the democratic debate (Wolterstorff & Audi, 1997). Marsden (1997) argues that this isn't copping out as Christians; it is simply recognizing that God calls us to different tasks in different spheres of our lives. We do have ultimate allegiance to God, but that allegiance includes making sure that all people, even those who reject God, receive public justice from the government. This public justice includes having room in the public square. Drawing from the justice commands of the Old Testament and the parable of the wheat and the tares in the New Testament, Christian political and legal scholar Bernard Zylstra put it this way:

> Because of sin the gods men love are many. And, for centuries, the lovers of God have denied the right of others to

love their god. If in Christ we know what it means to love God, do persons who claim to love god as revealed by Buddha or Mohammed have the right to the fulfillment of their claim? And what about the persons who claim that the god they are called upon to love is human personality itself? A just society may not discriminate between one religion and another. The wheat and the tares are allowed to coexist until God's final day of judgment. This does not mean that the social order is neutral with respect to religions. Societal orders ought to be so structured that a multiplicity of religions can flourish side by side. (Zylstra, 1991, p. 319)

The Relationship of Values and Community

If we are to prepare children for participation in civil society, we must first help students understand that each of us is born into community. Parker Palmer (1990) says that we often think of "community" as an outward structure, but in fact it is not. Deep within each of us, whether or not we recognize it, is something that compels us to care for each other. "Community is our created condition," says Palmer, and adds that our first task, then, is not to create community but to remember it and to help our students remember it (p. 149). Each of us must search deep within ourself to find at our core the self we have become before we can strive to be the self it is possible for us to be. We will find that while on the surface we may be nice, respectable people, deep within is a monster who is envious of others, a coward who fears failure, or a despot who wants absolute control of others.

Annie Dillard (1982) suggests that the only way to find personal and communal unity is to "ride the monsters all the way down" and discover ourself at our core. It is when we recognize the monsters inside ourself that we find we are just like every other ordinary member of the human family. We are broken, hurting people. Palmer says that our successes and distinctions are what set us apart from others, but knowing the worst of what we are brings us together and enables us to remember community.

While recognizing the monsters of the inner life for what they are may be a journey filled with peril, Palmer says this is a peril we cannot avoid if we are to be fully human and helpful to others. Therefore, we must go into the peril and journey through it. If I am a teacher, recognizing my own inner core for what it truly is allows me to fully understand the community that is possible in a classroom. It is only after I have been honest with myself about myself that I can invite my students to look closely at themselves, to "follow the monster down," and to recognize the community of which we are all a part. At that point the "company of strangers" no longer exists, and we become the community that we are. It is then that we may speak of the responsibilities and values that are important to people who live in community (Palmer, 1990 p. 152).

Teaching Values in Community

What values are commonly held as those that must be taught in a forthright manner? Why may these values be taught? Why may Christian teachers teach these values with integrity, and why must all teachers be required to do so?

Many values seen as worthy moral standards for a culture derive from the various histories of the people of that culture. At times these values continue to be followed even if the people no longer follow the underlying beliefs that were a part of that history. For example, such moral standards as honesty, respect for individuals, respect for those in authority, self-control, caring for those in need, tolerance, justice, caring for the environment, and stewardship of resources are Christian values. But they are also commonly accepted standards of people of many different beliefs. These standards or values are part of our historical documents, and North American students, whatever their culture, can understand and accept them without accepting the explicitly Christian worldview from which they come. These values harmonize with more than one worldview and may even stand as cultural leftovers from a worldview no longer overtly accepted (Joldersma, 1997). For a variety of reasons, school communities agree that teachers will teach these values and will do so without mention of a deity.

An important part of values instruction in a community involves helping students develop a conscience that will enable them to judge whether their own actions are right or wrong. Christian teachers can aid this development by keeping in mind that learning in the classroom should be directed toward the following goals:

1. Students should learn to unwrap their personal gifts, whether or not the students know the Giver. These gifts may be linguistic, mathematical, musical, spatial, bodily kinesthetic, social, or some other. The teacher must help students recognize their gifts and then help them develop the willingness and abilities to develop these gifts. Each student must learn the responsibilities that go with his or her particular constellation of gifts.
2. Students should learn to share each other's joys and burdens. Students must take responsibility for justice in the classroom and the school and for the learning, care, and nurture of each other. No matter how successful one student may be, there really is no success unless other students are succeeding and feel successful. Students must learn to rejoice in each other's successes as they do their own and to grieve with each other over burdens as they grieve over their own.

3. Finally, the entire climate of a classroom should be one of living in peaceful community. A school is a community, and the ethos of that community depends on how students act toward each other and how teachers and students relate to each other. (Stronks & Blomberg, 1993)

These goals may form the personal ideals of the Christian teacher in a public school classroom because Christian teachers recognize that all students, whether or not they know it, are made in the image of God. To be made in the image of God means, in part, that we live our lives in relationships. These relationships include relationships with family, classmates, community, the larger society, other creatures, and every other aspect of creation. Each of these relationships carries with it certain responsibilities. Helping students come to recognize these relationships and responsibilities is an important task for the public school teacher. Students need to understand their responsibilities to themselves, to others, and to the earth even when they do not know the Creator because they need these understandings if they are to be responsible citizens in a democracy.

Students learn these responsibilities in different ways. In learning about and developing the unique constellation of gifts they each have, students will come to understand their place in this world and the responsibilities that are a part of that place. In learning to find joy in other students' successes and to provide support for students experiencing difficulties, whether those difficulties are academic, social, or personal, students will come to realize the necessity of helping others in their community. Being part of a school community that works to promote good relationships among students, among teachers, and between students and teachers will help students come to know the responsibilities that fall to members of such a community. By seeing that the welfare of the community can, at times, take precedence over the rights of an individual, students will learn that compromise is part of living in a democracy. Keeping these relationships and responsibilities before students will help them compare their own actions with actions that best serve the welfare of the community. In that way students learn to distinguish between right actions and wrong actions, an important part of conscience development. In James Fowler's words:

> conscience both permeates and draws from such qualities as our manners of doing our work and conducting the business of everyday life, our loyalty and fidelity as members of groups and associations, our sense of capacity for imagining and keeping solidarity with generations yet unborn. (1992, p. 235)

Knowing these values and practicing them in the classroom community will form the basis for positive character development.

Character Development

It would be wonderful if all children came to school well on their way to having learned many of the components of positive character development. Unfortunately, that is often not the case. It is particularly necessary, therefore, that teachers at all levels understand which components of character development to teach and how these components can best be taught.

James Fowler (1992) describes the interrelated components of teaching character development in terms of using stories, actions, and discussion.

Stories

We have known for a long time that certain kinds of stories lead to an identification with characters. Stories that come to us from our families, our cultures, our nations, and our religious traditions provide us with a sense of identity and play a big part in shaping who we become. In school, teachers must help students reclaim these stories along with the history of their region and nation. They must tell these stories so vividly and compellingly that students develop a dedication to equality, freedom, and justice for all. They must include stories about people who were wrong in the way they acted toward others, something Fowler calls "dangerous memories" (Fowler, 1992, p. 243). In this respect, teaching for multicultural awareness is not just a politically correct thing to do. Rather, it is essential so that students can come to know each other's stories and understand the validity of other points of view. School is where students come to know the combined story of our stories.

Actions

Through personal interactions in the classroom and elsewhere, students learn a sense of duty and obligation toward others. When students live and learn in an environment that teaches that all must take responsibility for the learning and welfare of those around them, they will from their earliest years participate in actions of service. These actions would include listening to younger children practice oral reading, helping students who have difficulty with math problems or with studying, and participating in service activities outside the school. In this way students will learn that daily life consists of actions of duty and obligation.

Discussion

Fowler tells us that character formation includes a willingness to grow in our ability to understand another person's perspective. As students do so they begin to understand the part that moral reasoning and judgment play in the development of the conscience. Teachers will lead students into this awareness as they discuss events such as Dr. Martin Luther King's decision concerning nonviolent protests, President Truman's decision concerning the use of the atomic bomb, or President Roosevelt's decision to house Japanese-Americans in camps. Students will come to realize the importance of obtaining accurate information about people's lives if they are to attempt to describe the perspective of any group of people.

The Outcome of Character Development

Moral attitudes are the voices of conscience that are being developed through stories and through discussions concerning events in the news and discussions about classroom and school interactions. According to Fowler, the conscience can be divided into five components.

1. *Conscience of craft.* This aspect involves making a habit of doing tasks thoroughly and well. This means developing a sense of personal standards and an understanding of pride in a task well done.
2. *Conscience of membership.* The conscience formed for personal integrity in one's private life should also be a conscience suited for personal integrity in one's public life as a leader or member of a group.
3. *Conscience of responsibility.* This refers to the development of a sense of duty and obligation to others that leads one to keep promises and keep confidences.
4. *Conscience of memory* and *conscience of imagination.* These aspects lead to the "lure and pull and corrective power of the imagination, which, while faithful to the past, allows us to engage it critically and transformatively.

This is the imaginative faithfulness by which persons claim solidarity with and ethical responsibility for generations yet unborn" (Fowler, 1992, p. 239). By remembering the strength, courage, weaknesses, and suffering of those who are part of our story, we can keep faith with our inheritance. We do so by committing ourselves to helping others who are poor, afflicted, or oppressed.

By taking pride in doing tasks thoroughly and well, students come to respect themselves. By remembering heroes of the past, students learn to dream about the possibilities for their own lives. By learning to respect their membership in the class and in the school, they learn to trust their membership in that community. Our intention is that the development of these consciences will encourage students to hope, trust, and love.

The following design, which incorporates many of Fowler's terms (p. 241), shows that these different elements can lead students to develop the strengths of character and moral attitudes that are needed for citizens in a democracy.

Teachers can teach for the identified consciences through the use of stories, discussions, and actions, providing opportunity for the development of character strengths and virtues. The intention of such instruction is that students will develop genuine moral attitudes of hope, love, and trust. These moral attitudes are not just emotions or values but always carry with them a practical component that leads to constructive actions in the world around the student. The hope that should develop is a positive, realistic vision of the future that allows a student to dream possible dreams and act in a constructive way, taking the necessary steps toward that dream. Love, in this context, is a relationship that draws the student's focus away from the self and leads to actions that arise out of concern for others. The trust that we ex-

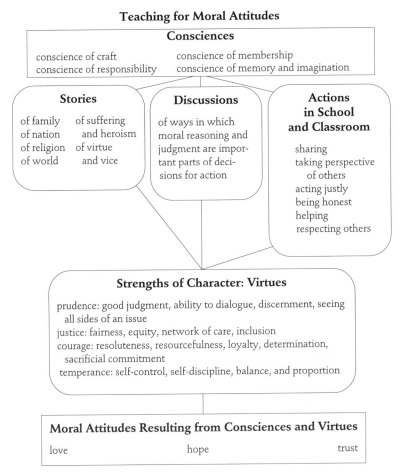

Teaching for Moral Attitudes

Consciences

conscience of craft

conscience of responsibility

conscience of membership

conscience of memory and imagination

Stories

of family   of suffering

of nation   and heroism

of religion   of virtue

of world   and vice

Discussions

of ways in which moral reasoning and judgment are important parts of decisions for action

Actions in School and Classroom

sharing

taking perspective of others

acting justly

being honest

helping

respecting others

Strengths of Character: Virtues

prudence: good judgment, ability to dialogue, discernment, seeing all sides of an issue

justice: fairness, equity, network of care, inclusion

courage: resoluteness, resourcefulness, loyalty, determination, sacrificial commitment

temperance: self-control, self-discipline, balance, and proportion

Moral Attitudes Resulting from Consciences and Virtues

love   hope   trust

Figure 1

pect will develop is an expectation of reliability that allows constructive actions to go forward.

Our hope is that through the use of stories, discussions, and classroom actions, teachers will not only challenge students to become discerning when evaluating the social structures that are in place but will also help them to have the commitment to take action when it is needed to transform social structures. A democracy needs citizens who not only can see what is right or wrong in the world but who are also willing to work for what is right.

As responsive disciples of Jesus Christ as well as responsible citizens in a democracy, we live between memory and vision. All of us live between the establishment of God's kingdom on earth with Christ's atoning sacrifice and its completion when Christ returns. Each new generation requires instruction in cultural meanings, instruction for its place within that culture, and instruction concerning an individual's responsibilities toward different aspects of that culture and toward other cultures. Teachers must know that it is not only their right but their obligation to teach the values commonly held in the larger society.

In some schools teachers are given specific curriculum materials designed for the teaching of character and moral attitudes. Other schools provide guidelines for this purpose, and the teachers plan ways to carry out the guidelines. Whichever the case, values and moral attitudes are best learned when they are interwoven into all aspects of classroom learning and school life. Curriculum planning with this in mind will be discussed in chapter 3.

3 Planning Curriculum

We have known for a long time that knowledge is never neutral. Whenever people teach, they do so from a perspective, a point of view or way of believing from which one views different aspects of the world. A teacher's perspective shapes the choices he or she makes when teaching, and therefore, it is tremendously important that teachers spend time reflecting on all that their particular perspective implies.

When we say that a teacher has a Christian perspective, we mean that the teacher holds to a set of beliefs that shapes his or her thinking. That does not mean, however, that all teachers who claim to be Christians will have exactly the same perspective. Each teacher is a finite creature with limited powers and abilities, and therefore, no one teacher can know perfectly. In addition, some teachers have deliberately thought about developing a Christian perspective while other Christian teachers have not.

Christians believe that the world around us is God's creation, whether or not people call it that. The world has a natural order that fills us with wonder and amazement because it is, to use a phrase of C. S. Lewis, like us, one of God's creatures. The world is ordered and structured by God, and God's people are to take care of the earth as a response to God's revelation. We cannot take care of what we don't understand, and therefore, understanding the world is our first response to God's revelation. God calls us to understand and then to act in keeping with that understanding (Hill, 1982). Holding these beliefs while teaching in a public school classroom does not mean that Christian teachers must isolate themselves from colleagues who hold different perspectives. True knowledge, which is God's knowledge, is built into the structure of creation, and therefore, different belief systems will overlap. As a result, professional partnerships can exist between Christian and non-Christian teachers, and they can share common concerns and learn from each other (Cooling, 1994, p. 161).

According to Trevor Cooling (1994), the central question that Christian teachers in public schools must keep before them differs from the question teachers in Christian schools must address. It is usually not helpful for a teacher in a public school to address the question: How can I integrate my faith with education in this school? This question treats public education as something that must always exist in its present form, as an ultimate given or as something sacred. Cooling believes it would be better for Christian teachers in public schools to ask themselves questions such as: How can my Christian beliefs be applied in this setting in a way that honors the educational needs of the children and the laws of the state? (p. 153).

The idea of applying one's beliefs may be troublesome, but this is what he means: Christians who teach in public schools may have the same perspective as their counterparts in Christian schools, but they know they must teach without evangelizing or proselytizing. It is important, therefore, that Christians who teach in public school settings search for ways in which their Christian beliefs can shape what they do in their classroom and in their school in ways that honor God, the educational needs of the children, and the laws of the state. Christian teachers need to think about

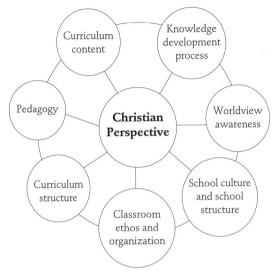

Figure 2

such things because, as Clarence Joldersma's illustration demonstrates, a Christian perspective influences the way a teacher thinks about every aspect of schooling.

In the education classes Joldersma teaches at Calvin College, he makes the point that when Christian teachers think about how knowledge develops, about matters such as classroom ethos, school climate, and curriculum content and structure, and when they plan how they will teach, they need to do so not as subversive agents bent on undermining the enterprise of the school but rather with an understanding about the nature of their task and the perspective they bring to that task.

Developing a Balanced Curriculum

Curriculum is the program of instruction found in schools. It specifies what will be taught and, to some extent, how it will be taught. Whether or not they admit it, many teachers and principals think of curriculum as simply a collection of subjects that are separate and distinct entities. The boundaries of these separate subjects are usually defined by the existing school schedule, the textbook selected for the course, and the teacher's loyalty to a particular area of study. While it may not be the most conducive to learning, this approach to curriculum is used in many schools.

What students need from the curriculum at any grade level, however, is a larger picture of their world and an awareness of how each issue or aspect they are studying fits into that larger picture. Curriculum that compartmentalizes subjects can keep students from seeing this larger picture.

In Christian schools, the purpose of curriculum is two-fold. First, through it students will come to know God's wonderful world with all its interconnections and will learn how to take care of that world. Second, the curriculum should help each student come to know his or her place in that world. In other words, students will come to know themselves and ways in which they, as individuals and as members of a community, stand in relationship to the rest of creation. This includes understanding the responsibilities that accompany one's relationships with family, school community, country, other creatures, and all aspects of the environment.

Christians who teach in public schools may have the same overarching goals in mind. They may desire to plan curriculum and teach so that their students come to know God's world and their place in it. At the same time, however, these teachers must keep in mind the goals of the school and the state or province. These goals include honoring the central purposes of the school, fulfilling the state or provincial mandates for a particular grade, teaching at a level that corresponds to the developmental level of the students, and addressing societal issues that are of immediate or long-range concern. Yet, both sets of goals can be met in such a way that neither is violated.

For example, Christian teachers can help students come to know about God's creation without mentioning God directly. Christian teachers believe that people are created to be curious. They are created this way so that they will come to understand much of God's marvelous creation. God wants us to know and understand creation because every aspect of it speaks of the one who made it. This knowledge of creation also makes students wonder about the purpose for things they cannot understand as well as for those they can. For example, scuba divers tell us that fish that live deep in the ocean look grey because the sunlight doesn't reach them, and therefore, their true colors cannot be easily seen. When one shines an underwater flashlight on those fish, however, their true, vibrant colors of neon red and luminous yellow become visible. When students see pictures of these fish, they may say, "I wonder why those fish are that way? Not many people will even have a chance to see them." Or when learning about kangaroos they might ask, "I wonder why the newborn baby kangaroo is so tiny and vulnerable while other animals are more fully developed when they are born. I wonder why God made the newborn kangaroo so different from other animals?"

Sometimes by serious study and careful watching, people can come to understand what the intended purpose for something is. Other times, however, it remains a mystery. Marjorie Grene (1968) reminds us that we know how the display of a peacock's fan functions in courtship. But the feathers of that fan contain an intricacy of patterns that seem to have no function at all. Why do those patterns exist if they aren't of any particular help to the peacock? She also tells of the black pattern on the wing of the mother-of-pearl butterfly. Although the size and background color are necessary for mating behavior, the beautiful, detailed black patterns that vary from one butterfly to the next have no known function. Further, the shells of sea snails are each unique and different, yet the variations and arrangements of colors have no significance for the snails. In fact, they don't even have eyes.

God made us curious in part so that we will want to know more about the world in which we live, and through our discovery, we will come to know God better. God also made us curious so that we will wonder about God and in our wondering we will praise God more, even when we don't find the answers to our questions. Information and attitudes such as these can be taught in a way without mentioning God at all. The Christian teacher can make the students aware of God's amazing creation without violating the goals of the school.

James Jadrich, a faculty member in the science department at Calvin College, describes this way of teaching as follows:

> When I teach science or design science curriculum at any level from kindergarten through college, my goal is usually to produce an integrated course, one that cuts across the traditional topics and disciplines found in science. The traditional topical approach to teaching science, which systematically and linearly covers topics and facts in life, earth, or physical science, leaves students with a compartmentalized view of nature. They acquire very little ability to see connections across the science disciplines and into other areas of life.
>
> On the other hand, an integrated science curriculum naturally ties the physical world together for students in ways that the traditional format cannot. An integrated curriculum uses the students and the surrounding environment as the starting point, and then it naturally addresses topics that are relevant and are more likely to be of interest to students. Questions such as "Why does my body feel the way it does?" or "Why won't my car start?" are examples of lead-in questions that start with the student and can only be answered by taking a wholistic or integrated view of science. Students learn

and retain information better when an integrated approach is used, and they see how all parts of nature are connected and are working together in harmony. They are left with a feeling of awe for the creation. Students also see that they are a part of the creation and that how they live and what decisions they make have an impact on all that is around them. They become responsible to and responsive to the creation.

However, providing students with a sense of wonder and awe about the creation is not the only goal of science education. In order to properly understand the universe and our ties to it, students must also become aware of the limitations of science. Without this awareness, students either obtain an inflated view of science and what it can do, or they are left with an inflated view of humanity. Therefore, throughout the curriculum and during the teaching, the teacher must emphasize the fact that science is a description of the physical world, but it is not an explanation for its origin and it cannot explain why nature is as it is. There are bounds to science. Questions that go beyond the bounds of science are worthy of contemplation, but science can shed little light into these areas. Therefore, a thoughtful appraisal of the limitations of science fosters humility, for it clearly shows that science can only address a single part of creation: the physical universe. Our values, what we value, and what is valuable are outside these limits. The scientist must remain humble, for he or she can only describe but a part of the creation. These limitations must be specifically addressed if we are to be fair to the students, fair to the discipline, and fair to the creation.

Finally, the curriculum and the teacher must emphasize the process of science, not just the facts of science, but how science is done as well. For the world was created for our benefit, and all of it is sacred—sacred in the sense that it is good and not evil. Therefore, no part of the creation is off limits to our study (although clearly some things should not be done). And as St. Paul says, the eternal and divine nature of God himself has been revealed in nature. Therefore, with the proper humility and wonder fostered as described above, even nonbelievers will obtain a glimpse of God in the science classroom as they do, and not just hear about, science.

(Jadrich, 1998)

Jadrich's description of helping students develop a sense of wonder and awe about creation while keeping in mind the possibilities and limitations of science is a beautiful example of how Christians can use an authentic voice when teaching.

The second purpose of curriculum is equally important. Christian teachers want their students to come to know their place in this world and to believe in the possibility of their own success. They want each student to be able to say, "I know the kinds of intelligences I have. I know my gifts and I know the responsibilities that go along with having these gifts. I am coming to know what I am to do and be in this world." Curriculum at any grade level should help students acquire a larger picture of their world, an awareness of how each issue or aspect they are studying fits into that larger picture, and an understanding of themselves in relationship to the world.

Diana Trotter, a faculty member at Whitworth College, describes her Christian perspective on the role theatre plays in helping students understand themselves and their place in the world:

Throughout history, theatre and the Christian church have had an uneasy relationship. The church frowns on the unorthodox lifestyle of the theatre artist and looks with a skeptical eye on the imaginative world of the stage. With the exception of the explicitly Christian theatre of the European Middle Ages, the church has viewed most theatrical endeavors at best with distrust and often with open hostility. Actors are hypocrites who create false realities and undermine biblical truth. Plays rouse violent passions and glorify characters and lifestyles antithetical to Christian morals. In turn, theatre scholars argue that religious subject matter makes for poor theatre and that so-called Christian drama is merely didactic propaganda. Both sides seem to believe that theatre, which by its nature raises questions, has little in common with a religion that claims to have all the answers. This mutual antagonism is surprising when one considers the fundamental questions at the heart of both the theatrical and religious impulse: What does it mean to be human? What is the meaning of our life on this earth? Is there something beyond what is immediately apparent? How do we make sense of the world? How shall we live our lives? What kind of society should we create? When framed by these questions, the study of theatre history and dramatic literature implicitly address the same concerns that form the foundation of what it means to live a Christian life, regardless of whether or not the theatre practice in question is itself explicitly "Christian."

The act of playing a character is the most controversial aspect of the theatre for the Christian church. Christians worry that actors will become tainted by the less than perfect characters they portray. Yet this ability to identify is the most valuable lesson the theatre offers for Christians. Christ calls us to love our neighbor as ourselves. We are to feed the hungry, shelter the homeless, care for the poor, heal the sick, and give hope to the oppressed. But how can we care for others if we do not know or understand them? Playing the role of an Other allows the actor to walk in someone else's shoes, look through someone else's eyes, experience life from someone else's perspective. Through acting, students step outside of their own experience and enact the circumstances of someone else. Students of acting learn not only technical skills but also compassion and empathy. While characters are fictional creations, they represent real people with whom audience members are certain to identify. As such, character study should be approached with love and compassion as an opportunity to develop sensitivity toward those who may be different from us. Acting also teaches us about our similarities and the ways in which all people are connected through their common humanity.

Creativity is one of God's greatest gifts to us and one of the ways we participate in reflecting God's image. Every great endeavor, from the creation of the world to the discovery of the atom, involves creativity and imagination. Faith itself is an act of the imagination. The ability to hope for what is unseen and to believe the seemingly impossible requires that we develop a creative, imaginative spirit. Theatre training that includes improvisation, interpretation, storytelling, and playwriting encourages that development. The world of make-believe, so often condemned by the early church, enables us to conceive the possibility of new and better ways of living our lives and points us to the existence of the transcendent.

Finally, theatre is the most communal of all art forms. Making theatre teaches students how to work together successfully toward a common goal and helps them develop important skills in group dynamics, leadership, and communication. As a collective, creative act, theatre can serve as a model for the way communities ought to live and work together. (Trotter, 1998)

Trotter's description of the theatre as a means to help students learn to identify with others and address some of the important questions of life is a wonderful example of a framework that provides guidance for a Christian teacher who is teaching in any setting.

As stated earlier, many Christian characteristics are also characteristics needed in a democratic society. Learning to take responsibility for one's own development, to respond appropriately to the joys and needs of others, to try to understand as much as possible about the world and to stand in wonder and awe about the parts one does not understand, and to live in harmony with others and with the world are not only characteristics of the Christian life but of the life of a responsible citizen in a democracy as well. A Christian teacher's reasons for promoting such a classroom and school environment will differ from those of other teachers, but the strategies for teaching and the observed outcomes may be the same.

A Framework for Curriculum

While Christian teachers may belong to many different religious denominations, they share certain basic beliefs:

1. God created the heavens and the earth and continues to be Lord of all creation.
2. God gave human beings a special place in creation. Therefore, humans are responsible for its development and care. People are created to be curious so that they will explore this creation, take care of it, and discover new aspects of it, always praising God for this marvelous work.
3. Human beings responded in disobedience and attempted to glorify themselves rather than God. This disobedience resulted in brokenness between humankind and God and also in many aspects of creation. The task of human beings has not changed as a result of this brokenness, but people continue to be alienated from God, nature, and each other.
4. God sent Jesus Christ, through whom the life-line between God and humankind was restored. Because of Jesus Christ, people can again take responsibility for the task of caring for God's world and healing that which is broken.
5. At the end of time, everything will be made perfect and sin will no longer exist.

These beliefs have provided direction for many Christian teachers in Christian schools as they help students understand their place in God's world. Together, these beliefs have come to be called the "creation-fall-redemption-restoration" motif. In attempting to teach with this motif in a Christian school, the teacher uses the following questions to provide a framework for discussion:

1. I wonder what God's intention was for this particular area of creation we are studying?
2. How has this purpose been distorted by the effects of sin?
3. What can we do to bring healing to the brokenness of this part of creation? What does it mean to treat this part of creation with integrity, in accordance with God's intention?
4. I wonder what this part of creation will be like when Jesus Christ returns and all things are made perfect?

These beliefs can also provide a framework or structure for the thinking of Christian teachers who teach in public schools. The questions, which would need to be modified, might follow this pattern:

1. If this part of the earth (whether soil, rain forests, communities, or most other topics being studied) were perfect, what might it be like?
2. What happened to make it imperfect?
3. What can we do to make this aspect we are studying closer to what it ought to be?
4. Try to describe how things would be different if this aspect of life were perfect.

Teaching with the "creation-fall-redemption-restoration" motif in mind should not be forced; it does not work with every topic. Many teachers, however, find it is a helpful way of thinking about teaching that is in keeping with their Christian faith.

Developing Christian Frameworks at the College Level

The statements of Jim Jadrich and Diana Trotter in an earlier part of this chapter help us understand how the Christian faith can shape the way teachers think about curriculum in the areas of science and theatre. Because this way of thinking about curriculum appears difficult, we wanted to know how college faculty in other disciplines allow their faith to shape the way they teach in a secular setting. Mathematics teachers often find it difficult to teach math from a distinctively Christian perspective, whether one is in a Christian or a public school. Richard Faber, a faculty member at Dordt College, provides the following explanation of how this can be done:

> How do you teach mathematics from a distinctly Christian perspective? Answers to this question are subtle. Since mathematics teachers cannot point to a particular theorem or algorithm that is different for Christians, it is tempting to think that Christianity is not as relevant to mathematics as it is to, for example, biology. A Christian biologist would teach that God created life, while a non-Christian biologist might say that there is a very small, but positive, probability that life spontaneously evolved on a given planetary system. Since this is an immense universe, the environment for evolutionary development was correct somewhere.
>
> How is mathematics taught from a Christian perspective without an analogous "creation/chance" example? The key is in one's perspective. Christians and non-Christian mathematicians may teach the same mathematics, however, their views on what mathematics is and how it interacts with reality are different. The biologists "creation/chance" example arises because they desire to understand how life began. If biologists never addressed such reflective questions, Christian biologists would find Christian biology just as nebulous as Christian mathematicians perceive Christian mathematics.
>
> In all math classes, instructors must decide which topics to include and which to eliminate. In most cases many valu-

able concepts may be dropped. This practice makes it very difficult to take time to step back and reflect with students on a comprehensive mathematical picture.

As Christians we know that God created and sustains an orderly universe. The created order makes it possible for mathematics to effectively describe many aspects of creation well. For example, the relationships between time, distance, velocity, and acceleration are modeled by functions, derivatives, and integrals. The temptation is to deify mathematics and to think that these mathematical concepts rule the motion of objects. However, the fact that these principles accurately explain creation is a testimony to God's faithfulness in creation. Through mathematics we use words and symbols to explain the creational order.

Much of mathematics is the study of the interdependence of structures and concepts of creation. Many structures and concepts in other disciplines have mathematical relationships. Mathematicians look for abstract ideas that contain the essence of the discipline-specific concepts. For example, derivatives and integrals help us understand disciplines ranging from economics to biology to engineering. These connections testify to the interdependence and structural beauty of creation. Mathematicians expect abstract mathematical concepts to have applications in initially unexpected areas. This revelation about creation is apparent to Christian and non-Christian mathematicians. However, the Christian understands this to mean that creation is unified, while a non-Christian may think that mathematics controls the universe.

Humans have a special place in creation. As the only image bearers of God, we are called to be stewards of creation. As stewards we must proclaim God's greatness by revealing the order and beauty of creation. Mathematics is a tool that helps us accomplish this goal. As image bearers we are creative beings. This aspect of our humanity is essential to our learning. To understand creation properly we need an abstract model that reflects the properties of our study. To understand something we recreate it in our minds. For example, to understand distances between places, we think of the

Cartesian plane and distances between points on a plane. The Cartesian plane is a human concept used to help us understand one part of God's creation. This concept proves to be very useful, but we know it is not a perfect way to measure distances on earth. The earth is mostly spherical and not flat. This illustrates that our mathematical descriptions are only a partial reflection of the actual creation. However, there is so much beauty and order in creation that even our partial reflections contain unending wonders. Mathematical responses to creation have been ongoing throughout history. The methods of mathematics and the thought that drives the development of mathematics have changed over time. One must include historical development in math courses to enable students to observe that mathematics is dynamic and that much of mathematics is a response to problems or questions about creation. To best understand mathematics one needs to understand the discovery of early mathematical theories and the progression of development. It helps to know how people thought about concepts initially and who raised mathematical understanding to higher levels. To appreciate the significance of Isaac Newton's Fundamental Theorem of Calculus (using antiderivatives to calculate area), students need to understand how areas were approximated before the seventeenth century by a "method of exhaustion." By calculating areas both ways students can understand how Newton radically changed mathematics. Mathematics teachers enable students to reflect and observe that their mathematics knowledge is a segment of a much larger mathematical structure. Christian teachers need to communicate that this structure is a creative response to God's universe. (Faber, 1998)

Steve Holtrop, on the education faculty at Huntington College in Ohio, proposes a framework for teaching that emphasizes responsibility.

Responsibility means purposeful education. It means education with an impact.

Such education is student-centered *and* subject-centered *and* teacher-centered in the sense that the responsibility is spread all around. We need responsible students who are taught by responsible teachers who use responsible materials and methods. Students take responsibility for their own learning. Teachers take their job as a divine calling to a fully professional endeavor. Curricular materials are not sugarcoated, censored, or vacuous and dry, nor are they merely politically correct. Responsibility implies stewardly protection and nurture. Schools are about taking care of ourselves, each other, and the setting in which God puts us. (Holtrop, 1997, p. 56)

Sharon Hartnett, a member of the education faculty at Whitworth College in Spokane, elaborates on the themes of responsibility and accountability. She states that these ideas can only be taught when students are taught by teacher-leaders who offer them love, hope, truth, and identity (Hartnett, 1997, p. 253).

Other college faculty who have taught on secular campuses provide insights concerning the way they integrate their faith with their teaching. Julia Stronks describes her approach to the discipline of political science in the following way:

Civics or government classes stem from the discipline of political science. In political science, the central question is this: What is the job of the state? This question is the same for Christians and for non-Christians alike. And because the answer to the question emerges from a person's view of what it means to be human, the different possible answers must be understood and explored by Christians and non-Christians alike.

I have taught introductory politics classes in Christian institutions and in public institutions. My faith provides me with certain truths that are foundational to my understanding of government in both settings. God is Lord of all creation, including the state, whether or not we choose to recognize this. The state's job is to do justice to all people and institutions of all faith traditions. Jesus never used the power of the state to convert people, and Christians today should follow the example of the farmer in Matthew 13. When the farmer's helpers saw the wheat and the weeds coming up together, they asked if they should separate the wheat from the chaff. The farmer said no. So the sun that shone, shone on both the wheat and the weeds. The rain that fell, fell on both the wheat and the weeds. The wheat and the weeds were not separated until the harvest. This means to me that when Christians talk about the task of government, they must ask what it means to have the public, civil equivalent of the parable's sun and rain providing equally for all people.

So when we talk about the role of the law, my students and I ask why we think certain activities should be legal or illegal. This leads easily into a discussion of different faith traditions' answers to the same question. When we analyze majority rule, we talk about the rights and obligations of all citizens in a nation. This leads easily into different faith traditions' perspectives of justice. And when we talk about the nature of representation, we examine the nature of obligation. When we talk about the identity of the nation state, we talk about the obligation of citizenship in the world.

In a Christian institution, my classes are specifically geared toward helping Christian students figure out what a biblical vision of the state could look like. Although I do not use biblical references in public institutions, I have never felt constrained in presenting Christian arguments about the state as the class examines liberal, socialist, feminist, or any other approach to the questions of the day.

Sherri Lantinga, who teaches in the psychology department at Dordt College, explains how she integrated faith with her teaching in a university setting that was hostile to Christianity:

I now teach at a Christian college, but I began my teaching career in a university setting that was hostile to Christianity. Despite this hostility, my beliefs still influenced the way I taught psychology. In my current setting, I have had the support to further think about the field of psychology from a Christian perspective. Upon reflection, I believe that my approach to teaching and my criticisms of psychology would not necessarily be unacceptable in a non-Christian setting. Indeed, many of the things I do in the classroom do not appear, on the surface, to be much different from what some of my non-Christian colleagues were doing. But my reasons for doing them were different, and I believe that these underlying reasons, though not explicit, were very important for my students' learning.

Perhaps most fundamental to my general approach to teaching is my belief that students are created as image bearers of God. As such, students should be treated with respect and dignity, as people responsible for making good choices and exercising self-discipline. The practical implications of this basic belief include (a) my learning and regularly using all of my students' names; (b) having high standards for students (e.g., no late assignments accepted); (c) giving constructive and prompt feedback on tests, papers, and other assignments; and (d) clearly writing out my expectations for assignments (e.g., providing sample papers, stating the criteria for how each assignment will be evaluated). I am continually amazed at the influence of these rather simple techniques on students' behavior. For example, I very rarely deal with issues regarding late assignments, but colleagues teaching different sections of the same course have the constant problem of discerning whether students' varied excuses for late papers are legitimate.

Emphasizing the development of communication and critical thinking skills is also not unique to Christians. However, for Christians, an emphasis on these skills stems from the realization that as communal creatures, the ability to communicate clearly with others is very important. In my classes, I require students to turn in multiple drafts of papers, take short essay exams, and to participate in small group discussions as a way of encouraging students to try to articulate what they are thinking. Relatedly, critical thinking skills learned in the classroom enhance students' discernment in a variety of domains outside the classroom. For example, the psychology of persuasion is particularly useful for developing critical thinking skills; I bring print advertisements to class to foster discussion of persuasion techniques and to teach students to look beyond the superficial characteristics of the ad.

Beyond my general philosophy of teaching, other beliefs influence how I teach psychology in particular. I believe that God created the world and everything in it, with people being the crown of the created order. People are relational creatures, and are therefore made with a built-in motivation to belong. This motivation makes psychology intrinsically interesting—we all want to understand how and why people behave the way they do. Although psychology textbooks and non-Christian colleagues do not acknowledge this motivation as part of our created natures, this human need to belong makes perfect sense to students and can be easily discussed without reference to an underlying Christian perspective. To promote an attitude of gratefulness and appreciation of mystery, I include as one of my course objectives the encouragement of students' wonder at the complexity of human behavior. To foster this goal, I include simple demonstrations during classes (e.g., personal space intrusions) and assign small research projects outside of class (e.g., observe your own and other reactions when you cut into a line) that make the textbook readings come alive for students. I find that as the course continues, students are eager to volunteer for demonstrations in front of class and that such demonstrations are almost certain to provoke questions and discussion (even if the demonstrations don't always work the way they should).

My Christian perspective has influenced not only my philosophy of teaching but also my perspective on psychology as a discipline. Teaching the methods or ethics of psychological research is a natural place to introduce the little-recognized problems in psychology as a social science (see Van Leeuwen's work for more on this). For example, psychological theories and research tend to overemphasize situational or biological factors that "determine" our behavior and disregard issues of personal responsibility and choice. Also, modern psychology is heavily dependent on experimental methods; such an approach limits the types of research questions that can be asked (we do not study what cannot be measured), and it is too often disrespectful in its treatment of people (subjects) both by using deception and by reducing humans to passive respondents observed in unnatural laboratory settings. Each of these problems, determinism and empiricism, can be used in discussion with students.

One way to begin discussion is to have students think of important human characteristics that are not very measurable (e.g., love, courage, religion). The discussion can then proceed to how those very things that we think of as defining humanity cannot be studied at all from a modern psychological standpoint. To engage students in discussion of the ethics of psychological experimentation, small groups can write an informed consent statement for a research study they have read about in their textbook. This assignment highlights for them the difficulty of truly informing research subjects but not revealing the experimenter's key hypotheses—that is, they learn firsthand about the deception that researchers must often use to conduct their research.

In short, teaching psychology from a Christian perspective includes many of the same techniques used by non-Christian teachers. However, the Christian teachers' thoughtful treatment and discussion of people as complex creatures worthy of respect and dignity is a unique contribution that is at the same time acceptable in non-Christian settings. (Lantinga, 1997)

Developing Christian Frameworks at the Elementary and Secondary Levels

Teaching with a "creation-fall-redemption-restoration" motif in an elementary or secondary public school may seem difficult at first, but teachers can be helped if they think in terms of important themes in the world around us that belong in the curriculum. Those themes might include the following: justice, community, identity, relationships, wellness, or intelligence. Maya brings these insights to teaching in the following way:

I teach eleventh graders in an inner city high school, and this is how I go about integrating my beliefs into my class work. I teach a two-hour block in the humanities. I began one fall term by drawing a circle on the chalkboard and telling the class that we would be designing a perfect community. It wouldn't have perfect people, mind you, but the community would be as perfect as we could possibly make it.

The students then set about planning this community. They had to decide whether a government was needed and, if so, what kind of government that would be. They needed to provide answers to questions such as: Would there be taxes and, if so, what kind? What kind of health support was needed and how would it be paid for? What kinds of transportation systems would be available and how would they be paid for? Would there be poor people in the community? Why or why not? How would they be taken care of? What kinds of schools would be available? Should education be compulsory and, if so, until what age? This took us quite a long time because, in order to plan what would be better, they had to know what presently exists. A great deal of research was needed.

Next, I assigned the part of Plato's *Republic* that describes utopia. The library had several copies on audio-cassettes for students who would have difficulty with the reading level. After the assignment was completed, we compared Plato's utopia with our own design for a perfect community. The students liked their own better but made some additional modifications at that point.

Our next step was to study the communities that the state guidelines said were to be part of our required curriculum. Communities of early American settlements are an important part of our curriculum at this grade level. We don't use one particular textbook, but there are many textbook copies and other resources in my classroom as well as in the library. With each community we identified how they had answered the questions we had raised about our own ideal community. We talked about what had gone wrong in the community we were studying and discussed ways things could have been changed for the better. Comparing their answers to our own helped the information become meaningful to the students.

However, you will remember that one January our country was engaged in the Gulf War. This class immediately dropped the community we were studying and began a study of Moslem communities both in the U.S. and in the Middle East, all the time comparing what we were learning to our original design for a perfect community.

Maya at no time talked about God nor about the Creator's plan for communities on earth. In describing her teaching she would not have used an expression such as the "creation-fall-redemption-restoration" motif. Nevertheless, she clearly planned instruction so that the class came to understand how things might be if they were perfect, what went wrong resulting in brokenness, and how people can work toward healing what has been broken. It is no surprise to learn that Maya is a devout Christian.

Other teachers find different ways of using this theme. Ann is a fourth grade teacher.

I use questions like that in teaching about the rain forests, but the sequence I use is different. I begin by using the K-W-L procedure to determine just what background knowledge my fourth graders have concerning this topic. I first of all ask what they know about rain forests. Then, together, we find out what it is they want to learn about them. Then the students research all the reasons why rain forests are important to us. The books and articles used for the research all lead them to understand that the rain forests are in danger. So we study to understand what the dangers are. That leads us very naturally to wanting to know what people could and should do to help the rain forests survive and flourish.

Chris, an art teacher, prepared the following unit for use with a fourth-grade class. Specifically, the unit concerns a garden with plant life, bugs and insects, and ponds.

Curriculum Unit: The Wonder of Our World

Theme or Organizing Center

The first purpose for the unit is that students will come to know God's wonderful world and all of its interconnections and will learn how to take care of that world. The second purpose is so that each student will come to know his or her place in that world. Students will see that they are part of creation and how they live and what decisions they make affect all that is around them. They will become responsible to and responsive to the creation.

Goals and Objectives

Goals

1. The unit will help students discover who they are and how they relate to creation.
2. The unit will provide each learner with experiences that promote personal growth.
3. The unit will provide experiences that impact learning and connect content to students.
4. The unit will appeal to students, will have the potential of addressing differences in student interests and abilities, and will be manageable.

Objectives

1. The learners will wonder, be curious, and appreciate the creation, the world that God has given to us.

2. The learners will know what happens when our world is broken (in the natural sense) and what we can do to preserve our world and develop a commitment to preserving our creation.

3. The learners will be able to express their wonder about creation in various art forms and connect their knowledge with the changing seasons.

4. The students will design their own gardens and describe what would be found in their garden (trees, flowers, bugs and insects, sculptures, ponds, etc.) using all the information they have collected in their journals throughout the year.

5. The students will depict their final project through a written piece, a painting or drawing, a diorama or three dimensional plan, or some other way. These projects will be displayed at our school's Celebration of Learning at the end of the school year.

Content, Concepts, Skills, and Attitudes

1. Students will explore the wonders of nature by exploring the different seasons and looking at the details of nature in each season using artwork and real examples in nature as their resources.

2. Students will keep a garden journal throughout the year—a place to keep their thoughts, lists, photos, and other information they will need to design their gardens in the spring.

3. Students will create a portion of a radial garden design after each season is studied. Students will record through their drawings what concepts they have learned about nature in each season. In the center the students will place a photograph of themselves or drawings of symbols that identify their particular interests in the garden.

4. The guiding questions for the unit will be:

   a. If this part of the earth (a garden) were perfect, what might it be like?

   b. What happened so that this is not perfect?

   c. What can we do so that this aspect we are studying would be closer to what it ought to be?

d. How would things be different if this aspect of life were perfect?

We will discuss these questions after each season is studied, and students can record their thoughts and answers in their journals. (The implementation plan for this unit, along with a sequence of lesson plans, can be found in Appendix B.)

Chris prepared this unit as part of her work in a graduate course in curriculum. In her own evaluation of the unit Chris said the following:

> This unit matches my worldview and my vision of how things are and how they ought to be. I use the four creation-fall-redemption-restoration questions in evaluating each lesson. The unit answers a faith commitment question (I have had), which is primarily how can I, a Christian teacher, teach the values and beliefs that are important to me in a public school setting. My primary commitment is a respect for God, other people, and creation.
>
> I believe this unit is life affirming for all students in that it not only promotes individual success but also promotes an awareness, wonder, and curiosity, and therefore, a commitment to respect our creation. The unit challenges students to think critically about nature and the seasons, to become discerners and transformers of our creation. It also fosters responsibility for learning because students are required to document their beliefs about nature and the seasons through their journals and artwork. I believe it fosters a discovery of personal talents and gifts because there are a variety of activities to help students discover their strengths and weaknesses in the eight multiple intelligences.
>
> Finally, I believe this unit allows for a change in attitude that includes an awareness toward nature based on new revelations and understandings that students will learn. (Hondorp, 1998)

Sonny, a grade four teacher taking the same course in curriculum, chose to create a unit on the topic "Geology: The

Earth and Its Changes." Sonny teaches in a charter school that recommends teachers use E. D. Hirsch's series as a guide, of which *What Your Fourth Grader Needs to Know* (1992) is a part. The curriculum content, therefore, is directly specified. Teaching in ways that are in keeping with the goals of a school and the benchmarks of the state might make a teacher feel there is little room for innovation, but this is not the case with Sonny. The lesson she teaches on the first day of this unit shows how she encourages her fourth graders to understand that their actions and thoughts are undergirded by basic beliefs.

On the first day of the geology unit, the students see a poster of the earth on the front marker board. Each child will be given a journal. I explain that throughout this unit they will be using this journal to write down their thoughts and questions, to record experiments, and to write creative stories and poems. Next to the poster on the board I have the very first journal prompt, which is, "People have many different beliefs about how the earth was formed and where the earth came from. What do you believe?"

I allow the students to write in their journals for ten minutes. When the ten minutes are up, we have a class discussion on the origin of the earth. I then present the theories of evolution and creation—all in a discussion format.

The assignment for day two is for the students to take their journals home and ask their families the same question. Family responses can be documented in the child's journal. (Huisman, 1998)

Susan Hasseler, who teaches the graduate curriculum course Chris and Sonny were taking at Calvin College, says that the most difficult aspect of planning curriculum in this way is finding the major life themes that make up the curriculum.

The toughest part of my curriculum theory class is challenging the participating teachers to determine the broad themes that undergird their curriculum and how those themes support or conflict with their worldviews. It is particularly difficult for teachers to step away from planning "neat activities" and begin to figure out what important concepts these daily activities are based on and what beliefs about teaching, learning, and the world these activities promote. When they do begin to look at curriculum this way, they express such wonder and excitement at seeing connections and meaning in the content they teach. It is a delight to be a part of that process. (Hasseler, 1998)

Clearly, it is not only children and adolescents who long to find meaning in what they do and in the world around them. Teachers find their own particular joy in teaching in ways that encourage students to understand the meanings that exist in God's world, even when the name of the One who created and maintains that world may not be mentioned.

Teaching Christianly in a public school classroom, while at the same time obeying the laws that govern such institutions and that protect the rights of all people, is possible, but it can only be done with careful thought. Singing the Lord's song in a strange land always requires careful reflection.

4 Religious Freedom and the Law

Most Americans are familiar with the phrase "separation of church and state." However, few people know what the phrase means. May a teacher mention his faith to his students? May children pray silently before lunch? May a public school coach cross herself before a game? In the follow-up to the Christians in Public Schools Survey, we found that the majority of the respondents believe it is legal for them to talk about religion in class. Because the concept of the separation of church and state makes the rules about this discussion so difficult, however, they often avoid mentioning faith in order to play it safe. The following information should shed light on this often complex issue, allowing Christian teachers to teach with more confidence.

The Law

There are four sources of law that determine the rights of religious people in public schools: (1) the First Amendment of the federal Constitution; (2) state constitutions; (3) the state laws that are developing in response to the failure of the federal Religious Freedom Restoration Act; and (4) the federal 1984 Equal Access Act.

Understanding the interplay of these laws is complicated, but it is important for everyone who works in the public arena to be familiar with the rules that protect and restrict the expression of faith. Public school teachers possess religious freedom, but they are also responsible to protect the religious freedom of students in their classes. Over the past fifteen years, parents of public school children have become more assertive in demanding the protection of religious expression in public schools. This means that avoiding the topic of religion, or playing it safe, is no longer a viable option.

The First Amendment

The First Amendment to the U.S. Constitution provides that "Congress shall make no law respecting an establishment of religion, or prohibiting the free exercise thereof; or abridging the freedom of speech." The first clause of the amendment is referred to as the Establishment Clause; the second part of the amendment is referred to as the Free Exercise Clause. Taken together these clauses mean that public schools must protect the religious exercise and expression of both teachers and students. However, public schools must also make certain that their actions do not establish a religion. Tension exists between these two directives of the First Amendment because vigorous protection of one person's right to exercise religious belief can be interpreted by others as an improper establishment of religion.

This tension can be most clearly seen in the debates concerning school prayer. If a school protects a Christian teacher's right to pray out loud before meals, the parents of non-Christian students will claim that the school is establishing a religion. If, on the other hand, the school fails to protect a Christian student's right to pray before a meal, the parents of the child will claim that the school is hostile toward religion, or even that the school is establishing a faith of secularism.

The tension between protection of religious expression and protection against establishing religion affects almost every part of public school life. Should science teachers be allowed or required to teach creationism? Should students be allowed to have a Bible club? May teachers wear artifacts of their religious tradition? Should a Christian theatre group be allowed to present a production during student assembly? Because the tensions within the First Amendment are inherent to the Constitution, it is difficult for teachers and school districts to know how to solve these everyday conflicts. As a result, most of these conflicts have resulted in some type of litigation. The decisions handed down by judges in these past cases give us guidance as to how to handle religious freedom conflicts.

Although the Supreme Court has been criticized for being inconsistent in its handling of religious freedom cases, in recent years the Court has been clear about a number of things. First, government, including the public school system, has an obligation to accommodate religion wherever possible. Second, religious speech should receive the same protection as other speech. Third, the classroom is supposed to be a "marketplace of ideas" (Whitehead, 1994). Although schools have a legitimate role as inculcators or transmitters of values, schools may not quash minority voices. In general, the Court has held that government may not establish one religion, may not establish any religion over any other religion, and must allow for citizens to exercise their own religion. Government must remain neutral to religion. But what do these phrases mean? At different times, the Court has emphasized different aspects of these constitutional principles.

In the past, the Court has held that accommodation of religion means that government *must* allow religious exemptions from laws that burden the exercise of religion. So when students are required to salute the flag in public schools, exemptions must be provided for students who have a religious objection to the saluting of the flag. In addition, the Court has held that government *may* accommodate religion to an even greater extent, as long as the Establishment Clause is not violated. This means that in some cases, even if the Constitution does not require it, school boards have the ability to choose to protect religious exercise of students and teachers. For example, the Constitution does not *require* school boards to pay public school teachers for leaves associated with religious holidays; however, the Constitution does *allow* school boards to pay for these leaves, at the board's discretion.

Unfortunately, it can be difficult to determine when accommodation is required, when it is merely allowed, and when it is prohibited because it would violate the Establishment Clause. In 1971, the Court developed a three-part test, referred to as the Lemon test, to determine when accommodation of religious belief violates the Establishment Clause (*Lemon v. Kurtzman,* 1971). If the action of the government is to be considered constitutional, it must have a secular legislative purpose, its principal or primary effect must be one that does not advance or inhibit religion, and it must not foster "an excessive government entanglement with religion." Therefore, government policies that only incidentally foster religious belief are held to be constitutional. Under this test the reference to God in the Pledge of Allegiance was not considered an establishment of religion, particularly because students were allowed exemptions from saying the pledge if they objected to the words.

However, the Lemon test has proven to be a difficult test to apply because it is difficult to determine when "excessive" government entanglement exists. In 1984, Justice Sandra Day O'Connor suggested a new test to replace the Lemon test. She recommended that government actions be ruled invalid if they create a perception that government is either endorsing or disapproving of religion. In other words, does the challenged governmental action give a message to non-adherents that they are outsiders or a message to adherents that they are insiders?

A few years later, Justice Anthony Kennedy suggested an alternative to Justice O'Connor's approach. He stated that the real question should be whether the government action coerces individuals to be involved in religious activity. If not, then the government action should be allowed. This is the test that was used in the case that ruled clergy-led graduation ceremony prayers unconstitutional. Kennedy said that even subtle pressure can act as compulsion. Because students sitting in an auditorium are forced to listen to the prayer, they are indirectly coerced into participating in the prayer. Unfortunately, although the other justices on the Supreme Court agreed with Kennedy in this case, they divided on the issue of whether "coercion" is necessary before violation of the Establishment Clause occurs. Some justices believe that government action is unconstitutional only when direct coercion occurs; some justices believe that government action is unconstitutional when either direct or indirect coercion occurs; and still other justices believe that endorsement, not coercion, violates the Establishment Clause (Whitehead, 1994).

State Constitutions

As complicated as the federal case law is, the law surrounding protection of religious exercise becomes even more difficult when considering state constitutions. Many states, particularly those in the West, have provisions in their constitutions that restrict religious activity in the public arena even further. Today, state law is widely recognized as providing another level of argument concerning the meaning of religious freedom.

Interpreting the decisions handed down by the U.S. Supreme Court and the supreme courts of different states is difficult even for legal experts. But this does not mean Christians should throw up their hands in despair. Over the last twenty years, legislators have paid more attention to the confusion in the case law. Now the federal and state governments are trying to clarify the rights and responsibilities of religious people in public schools.

The Religious Freedom Restoration Act: The Fight Isn't Over

Even though the Constitution protects the free exercise of religion, religious freedom rights are not absolute. In fact, no constitutional rights are absolute. Over the past century, the Supreme Court has devised tests to help determine when government may limit rights that are clearly expressed in the Constitution. If the government wants to limit a right such as speech, equal protection, or the exercise of religion, it must pass the strict scrutiny test. In other words, the government must show that it has a compelling state interest, a compelling reason to limit the right. Furthermore, the government must show that it has taken the least restrictive means possible to achieve its goal. If the government cannot persuade the courts that it has met this high test, the government regulation limiting the constitutional right will be declared invalid and unconstitutional.

For decades the strict scrutiny test was applied to free exercise cases. The result was that religious freedom was often protected. In the school systems this meant students were exempted from activities that they felt hindered their ability to be faithful to their beliefs. However, in 1990 the Supreme

Court handed down a much criticized decision. The Court ruled that if a law burdened religious exercise but appeared to be neutral to religion, in other words, the law seemed to apply equally to everyone, that law would not be subject to the strict scrutiny standard but rather a lower standard of scrutiny. Rather than being required to show a *compelling* state interest, government would have to show only that it had a *reasonable* state interest in limiting the constitutional right of free exercise of religion.

This case produced an outcry from many groups and was the catalyst for the development of a broadly based coalition of religious and civil rights groups. This coalition worked to develop the Religious Freedom Restoration Act (RFRA), which stated that government may "substantially burden a person's exercise of religion" only if it passes the compelling interest test. The act gave religious groups greater protection than did the 1990 Supreme Court ruling. In fact, the act "restored" the rights of religious persons by advocating the pre-1990 approach to the limitation of constitutional rights. The act was passed by the House and Senate in 1993 and was signed into law by President Clinton in November 1993. However, the law's constitutionality was tested, and in 1997 the Supreme Court declared it unconstitutional as applied to state laws.

The reason the Court found the law to be unconstitutional had more to do with federalism and states' rights than with religious freedom jurisprudence. This means the story of the RFRA is not yet over. The law the Court ruled unconstitutional was a federal law, but the Supreme Court left room for states to develop their own local RFRAs. Because state-based interest groups are currently working behind the scenes to encourage state RFRAs, it is important for teachers and school districts to be aware of possible state requirements.

If a state passes a local RFRA, a school district within that state has the difficult task of interpretation. The effect of the RFRA is not completely clear because "compelling state interests" are not always easy to define. Furthermore, the act applies only when a person's exercise of religion is "substantially" burdened, and it is not always clear when this occurs. But it is clear that the compelling state interest standard is difficult to meet and that in the face of it, government regulations are often declared unconstitutional. For school districts this means it is wise to attempt to accommodate requests of religious persons. In fact, the National School Boards Association Council of Attorneys [NSBA] has said that accommodation of faith-based requests is always preferred when the requests are not costly, dangerous, or educationally unsound. The key word is *balance*. If a school claims it has an interest in limiting a request by a person of faith, great effort should be put into figuring out whether there is a way in which the interests of the school and the religious concerns of the student or teacher can both be met.

The Equal Access Act

The Equal Access Act is a federal law passed in 1984 that prohibits schools from discriminating against students on the basis of the content of the students' speech. The act specifically provides that if a school maintains a "limited open forum" during noninstructional time, that forum must be open to all lawful religious, political, and philosophical voices.

> It shall be unlawful for any public secondary school which receives Federal financial assistance and which has a limited open forum to deny equal access or a fair opportunity to, or discriminate against, any students who wish to conduct a meeting within that limited open forum on the basis of the religious, political, philosophical, or other content of the speech at such meetings. (Equal Access Act, s4071(a), 1984)

The act applies to any school that qualifies as a secondary school, and according to the act, a "limited open forum" occurs when a school allows noncurriculum related student groups to meet on school premises during noninstructional time. Normally, public schools are considered closed forums. This means a school can control the meetings that take place on its campus and can limit those meetings to those related to the formal curriculum of the school. However, if the school chooses to allow students to conduct noncurriculum-related meetings during noninstructional hours, that school may not discriminate against the students on the basis of the content of their meetings. For example, scuba clubs, chess clubs, and service clubs are most likely not related to the curriculum of a school. If a school allows these clubs, it must also allow Bible clubs. However, a French club and student government organizations are most likely related to curriculum. If the school allows only these sorts of clubs, it may deny Bible clubs.

Generally, the act requires that the school apply the same rules and protections to student meetings of a religious nature as it applies to any other noncurriculum-related student meeting. But it is important to note that the protection of this act extends only to student initiated clubs. Teachers may be present during the student meetings to keep order, but they may not influence the form or content of religious activity. Teachers must be "nonparticipants."

A Growing Consensus?

The bipartisan support of the RFRA and the developing protections by the Supreme Court are two factors that suggest we are embarking on a new era in religious freedom jurisprudence, particularly as applied to public schools. In 1995, President Clinton took further steps to ensure that public school districts protect religious voices. He directed the secretary of education, in consultation with the attorney general, to inform school districts that according to the Department of Justice and the Department of Education, public schools were not to be "religion-free zones." Clinton and the Departments of Justice and Education set forth the following principles to supplement the Supreme Court decisions and to guide public schools in their decision-making processes.

- Students' prayers and religious discussions are to be protected. Students who desire to pray or to talk about religious issues have the same right to engage in these activities as do students who desire to engage in any other comparable nondisruptive activity. Although schools may impose rules of order, they may not discriminate against religious activity or speech, even if the activity is proselytizing. Students may not, however, engage in religious activity when they have a captive audience.

- Although teachers may not solicit or encourage religious activity, they may not discourage it, and they may not encourage antireligious activity.

- Students may express religious beliefs in homework, artwork, and other written and oral assignments.

- Students may distribute religious literature to the same extent that they are allowed to distribute other literature unrelated to school curriculum.

- Schools have great discretion in choosing to allow a student to be excused from activities or classes that are objectionable to the student or the student's parents. Schools must excuse a student from classes or activities if attendance in those classes would "substantially burden" the student's free exercise of religion (subject to the compelling interest test).

- Schools may actively teach civic values and virtues and the "moral code that holds us together as a community." The fact that these moral codes coincide with the teaching of specific faiths does not make the teaching of moral codes unlawful.

- Students may wear religious messages on their clothes to the same extent that schools allow students to wear clothes with other written or symbolic messages. If an article of clothing is required by a student's religion, schools may not prohibit that article of clothing (subject to the compelling interest test).

- The Equal Access Act's reference to "noninstructional time" includes recess and lunch periods as well as before and after school.

- The Equal Access Act requires equal access to means of publicizing meetings. If the school media, including the public address system, the school newspaper, and the bulletin board, are used by students to publicize noncurriculum-related student meetings, the school must allow religious student groups the same access to these means of publicity. (Riley, 1995)

The courts, the executive branch, and the legislative branch are all working to further clarify the rights and responsibilities of religious people in the public arena. This is clearly a good sign for Christian teachers committed to teaching in ways that are authentic to their faith commitments.

5 Applying the Law in the Classroom

Even though in recent years the Supreme Court has been clearer about the laws governing the protection of religious voices, school boards and school districts are at times reluctant to acknowledge religious freedom rights.

In 1985, the year after the Equal Access Act was passed, some high school students in the state of Washington asked their principal if they could meet on school grounds for informal Bible study before school. Although the school had a limited public forum policy, the principal denied the request. It took ten years of expensive litigation and a judgment against the school to convince the school's administration that the Bible study was a legitimately protected religious activity. On the other hand, sometimes school boards and school districts flagrantly violate the Establishment Clause of the First Amendment by broadcasting prayers through a school's public address system.

First Amendment religious freedom jurisprudence is developed through litigation. However, litigation is expensive, time-consuming, and often destructive to communities. The first section of this chapter explains the process that leads to litigation, showing how lawsuits can be avoided.

Minimizing the Possibility of Lawsuits

People use the courts to litigate their claims when their voices are not heard, when they are angry, or when they feel they have no choice. While litigation costs a great deal of money, civil rights cases are often funded by interest groups. Access to the legal system is not, therefore, as difficult as one might think.

Thirty years ago administrators could avoid lawsuits by avoiding the protection of religious liberty. People sued when they were exposed to religious beliefs that were antithetical to their way of thinking. Today, however, parents are more assertive about protecting the religious expression of their children. In the aftermath of the development of the religious right, lawsuits come from both sides. Today, silence about religion is an invitation to a lawsuit; it is not the means to avoid a lawsuit. As a result, schools have to be proactive in developing clear policies to deal with the inevitable conflicts that will arise over alleged violations of the First Amendment's Free Exercise Clause or its Establishment Clause. In developing policies, teachers and school districts should keep in mind the following guidelines expressed by Charles Haynes and Oliver Thomas in *Finding Common Ground.*

A school is supposed to be a "marketplace of ideas." A school, therefore, should include all voices when trying to resolve a conflict that involves debate about how life should be lived, and emphasize to parents that the school is trying to function in a pluralistic society in which people have competing value commitments. In setting "ground rules," Haynes encourages schools, teachers, and parents to keep in mind three Rs:

> Rights: Religious liberty, or freedom of conscience, is a precious, fundamental and inalienable right for all. Every effort should be made in public schools to protect the conscience of all students and parents.

Responsibilities: Central to the notion of the common good, and of greater importance each day because of the increase of pluralism, is the recognition that religious liberty is a universal right joined to a universal duty to respect that right for others. Rights are best guarded and responsibilities best exercised when each person and group guards for all others those rights they wish guarded for themselves. The Williamsburg Charter calls this "the Golden Rule for civic life."
Respect: Conflict and debate are vital to democracy. Yet if controversies about religion and schools are to reflect the highest wisdom of the First Amendment and advance the best interest of the disputants and the nation, then how we debate, and not only what we debate, is critical. (Haynes & Thomas, 1996, p. 5.2)

When curricular conflicts arise, start at the point of agreement. Then, when faced with a point of disagreement, the parties involved can discuss a variety of ways to handle it. Sometimes disagreement can be headed off with a simple change in the way we articulate an issue. Some schools have found that discussion of sexual abstinence is easier when the approach is not "teaching abstinence is good" but rather "what are the different ways we can teach about sexual abstinence?" In difficult situations, there are at least three viable ways to handle controversial issues:

1. Use different tracks for students to pursue different approaches to an issue. Let a child's parents decide which track is appropriate for their child.
2. Excuse students whose parents object to a particular piece of the curriculum.
3. Teach the controversy, showing students that there are a plurality of approaches to those issues on which we have no consensus.

Make sure the policies of the school are clearly communicated to everyone in the community. Litigation arises most often when people thought their perspective would be handled in one way, but in reality it was handled much differently. If the policies are clear, parents will be less likely to feel that their views were shut down without a hearing. Stephen Bates (1996) sets out further "tips" to help teachers and administrators who are confronted by parents who have complaints about book choices or assignments.

1. To preempt some protests, solicit community input before books are chosen.
2. Put in place a written procedure for dealing with complaints.
3. When a protest does arise, focus on how the public participated in the book selection.
4. Keep in mind both sides of the public schooling paradox: The curriculum must reflect the will of the community. [He points out that while truth is not a matter of majority will, curriculum is.]
5. Recognize that context does not erase all offenses. [Some parents will want their children excused from exposure to even brief racial epithets or profanity.]
6. Remember the civic obligation to respect freedoms of belief, speech, and religion, even for people with whom you disagree.
7. Church-state separation is an issue with sectarian material, too, if the protesters want sectarian material in the classroom, if they want teachers to make religious judgments on their behalf, or if they want to remove material solely because it conflicts with their religious beliefs.
8. When parents are seeking an alternative assignment, don't accuse them of misconstruing the assignment or its impact on students.
9. When parents request an alternative assignment, the school system should respond privately.
10. Recognize, and show that you recognize, that the protesters want what they believe to be best for the children.
11. Resist the temptation to engage in name-calling.
12. Remember: Obnoxious people have rights, too. (p. 5.7)

Legal experts agree that it is risky and difficult to be proactive when it comes to the issue of religious freedom in public schools (Haynes & Thomas, 1996). It is even riskier, however, to avoid discussing the issue. Lawsuits are expensive, and they can harm communities by creating almost irreparable damage. To the extent possible, teachers and school administrators should anticipate areas of possible conflict and do everything in their power to educate the community to handle cultural conflicts in ways that promote civic accord in a pluralist society.

The Law Applied

Court decisions that make up the body of laws governing religious freedom can be confusing. However, it is possible to glean some guidance from the cases handed down over the years.

Sometimes the law *requires* protection of religious expression; sometimes it merely *allows* it. Conflict can exist between what a teacher wants to do and what the principal or board allows. Conflict can also exist between what the board wants and what the law allows. Christian teachers need to know the parameters of the law so that they can encourage principals and boards to extend the greatest religious liberty protections allowed by the law. The following guidelines can be helpful in discerning a legal response to various situations.

- In general, religious expression in colleges and universities is more protected than religious expression in secondary schools.
- Religious expression in secondary schools is more protected than religious expression in elementary schools.

- Religious expression in nonmandatory school forums is more protected than religious expression during class periods.

With these general principles in mind, we can now address the specific rules that provide answers to the questions teachers may have.

Questions Teachers Ask

The answers to the following questions are based on U.S. case law, a document drafted by the National School Board Council of Attorneys (NSBA), and a joint statement of law on religion in public schools prepared by a coalition of sixteen American educational, religious, and political groups. For further information, we recommend that teachers purchase and consult the book, *Finding Common Ground: A First Amendment Guide to Religion and Public Education* by Charles Haynes and Oliver Thomas.

May I acknowledge religious holidays in my classroom?

Yes, but *celebrating* these holidays is not permissible. You must also remember that your discussion of religious holidays may not sponsor, advance, or inhibit religion. One federal court stated that religious holidays may be recognized if the purpose is to provide secular instruction rather than to encourage religious practices. As a result, if your discussion is integrated into your curriculum and it examines holidays of the different faith traditions in a pluralistic society, it will pass constitutional muster.

Religious holiday symbols may only be used on a temporary basis as a teacher aid when they are part of an academic program. Teachers should neither encourage nor discourage students to create artwork with these symbols. The NSBA states that teachers should even avoid asking students to explain their beliefs and customs. If a student volunteers this information, teachers should treat the offer to share beliefs in the same manner they treat opinions offered by students on other topics.

When trying to decide which seasonal activities would be appropriate, teachers should test themselves by asking the following questions:

Will this activity serve an educational purpose for all students?

Will this activity make students feel excluded if they do not profess any faith?

Will this activity make students uncomfortable because they are being asked to identify with a faith that is not their own?

Haynes uses another helpful set of questions:

1. Do I have a distinct educational purpose in mind? If so, what is it? It should not be the purpose of public schools to celebrate or observe religious holidays.
2. If I use holidays as an opportunity to teach about religion, am I balanced and fair in my approach? If I teach about Christmas and Easter, for example, do I also teach about non-Christian holidays?
3. Does the planned activity have the primary effect of advancing or inhibiting religion? Does it, for example, promote one faith over another or even religion in general? Remember that the school's approach should be academic not devotional. It is never appropriate for public schools to proselytize. (Haynes & Thomas, 1996, p. 10.7)

The NSBA, Haynes, and other religious and educational organizations suggest the following guidelines for school districts:

- Develop policies about the treatment of religious holidays in the curricula and inform parents of those policies.

- Offer pre-service and in-service workshops to assist teachers and administrators in understanding the appropriate place of religious holidays in the schools.

- Become familiar with the nature and needs of religious groups in the school community.

- Provide resources for teaching about religions and religious holidays in ways that are constitutionally permissible and educationally sound. (*Religion, Education and the U.S. Constitution,* 1994, p. 161)

These provisions may be easier said than done, but they indicate that individual teachers may legally discuss religious holidays in the classroom. Teachers should encourage their administration to recognize this and to provide appropriate legal guidelines.

Thomas provides a helpful summation of the issue:

A common misconception is that it is permissible to promote Christianity at Christmas provided that other religions receive similar treatment at other times. For example, some teachers may try to justify celebrating Christmas by celebrating Hanukkah. This approach is wrong. First, Hanukkah is not a major Jewish holiday and should not be equated with Christmas, one of the two most important holidays in the Christian year. Second, one violation of the First Amendment does not justify another. If it is wrong to promote religion in the public schools at Christmas, it is wrong every other day of the year. Instead of "balancing" Christmas with Hanukkah, teachers should work to ensure that all holiday activities focus on objective study about religion, not indoctrination. (Haynes & Thomas, 1996, p. 10.7)

What is permissible regarding Christmas and Halloween?

Christmas has presented a particularly difficult issue because it is acknowledged in the culture at large. The NSBA states that although holiday concerts may include religious music, it should not "dominate" the program. Dramatic productions should emphasize culture not faith traditions. Acknowledging Halloween calls into question the establishment of religion. Some people believe that when schools hold parties on Halloween, they are promoting the religion of witchcraft. The courts have not found that Halloween has religious overtones. Most schools, however, handle this holiday by allowing students to be excused from class if they have religious objections to the celebration.

May I tell my students that I am a Christian?

First, ask yourself this question: What is my purpose in sharing my belief system? If your purpose is to provide an avenue of conversion for students, you will be tempted to cross the legal line into encouraging or soliciting religious belief. However, if you are responding to a direct question from a student, and if your answer is short and to the point and relevant to the academic discussion at hand, it is allowed.

Outside the classroom, teachers may discuss religious beliefs with students as long as such discussions are student initiated and the student is never compelled to continue the discussion or to accept the teacher's beliefs. The law will balance the student's right over the teacher's right in these cases, so teachers are encouraged to err on the side of caution.

If a student asks a teacher to pray with him or her, the teacher should talk to the student's parents. There is nothing that clearly prevents a teacher and student from praying together during noninstructional time, but for a teacher to do so against a parent's wishes could be seen as coercive, even if it is at the student's request. There is currently no legally recognized right for a teacher to pray with or in front of students (Whitehead, 1994).

What limits are legitimately placed on my religious expression during nonclass time?

Teachers and school administrators, when acting in those capacities, are representatives of the state and, in those capacities, are prohibited from encouraging or soliciting student religious or antireligious activity. Similarly, when acting in their official capacities, teachers may not engage in religious activities with their students. Teachers, therefore, may not take part in prayer or worship opportunities that take place on many public school campuses. They may, however, engage in private religious activity in faculty lounges (Religion in the Public Schools, 1995, p. 3).

May I sponsor an after school Bible club?

Yes, but you may not initiate it. If students start a Bible club during noninstructional hours, the Equal Access Act is triggered (see chap. 4). Assuming that the school has a limited open forum and the students ask you to be their sponsor, the school must grant this request, but only if it is the school's policy to have teachers sponsor noncurriculum-related clubs. Whether or not you are a sponsor, you may attend the meetings at the students' invitation, but you must be a nonparticipant. You may not influence the religious study or activity of the students.

Off school grounds you may conduct Bible studies and invite whomever you wish. However, you may not use your position as a teacher to encourage students to attend.

May we have religious books in the public school library?

Yes. School boards may remove books from libraries only if the books lack educational suitability or contain pervasive vulgarity (Whitehead, 1994). School boards do have more control, however, over the selection of books for the library. Courts have found that the cultural role the Bible has played in history makes it a legitimate addition to any school library. The presence of religious books in a public school library does not violate the Constitution, but the absence of religious books also does not violate the Constitution.

May we have a moment of silence in class?

Yes. However, a great deal of litigation has taken place concerning moments of silence. If there is even a suggestion that the silence is really for prayer, it is not allowed. School districts' approaches to this issue vary tremendously.

May students evangelize on school grounds?

Yes, subject to consideration for others. The NSBA states:

Students have the right to speak to, and attempt to persuade, their peers about religious topics just as they do with regard to political topics. But school officials should intercede to stop student religious speech if it turns into religious harassment aimed at a student or a small group of students. While it is constitutionally permissible for a student to approach another and issue an invitation to attend church, repeated invitations in the face of a request to stop constitute harassment. (Religion in the Public Schools, 1995, p. 7)

Students may even distribute religious literature to their classmates if the school allows the distribution of political or other "viewpoint" literature.

May I invite a pastor to speak on a topic in my classes?

Yes. As long as the school has a policy that allows non-school speakers into a classroom, the school may not discriminate between speakers based on the content of their views. Schools must be viewpoint neutral, but they may limit speakers with respect to profanity and proselytizing. Schools may also set criteria concerning the acceptability of speakers (e.g., speakers must have firsthand knowledge of the topic at hand, speakers must be affiliated with an organization that is directly connected to the topic to be discussed, and so forth). The rules must, however, be applied evenhandedly to all speakers. Religious speakers may not be discriminated against. In like manner, however, teachers should not appear to discriminate against nonreligious adherents. Balancing pastors with other speakers will help you build an environment that welcomes discussion of all points of view and will help you fulfill the school's responsibility to be "viewpoint neutral."

May I add to or skip parts of the curriculum that the school board has agreed on?

Not really, but often teachers enjoy a great deal of freedom in this area. State laws and school boards control curriculum, but they do not have unlimited control. Teachers are constitutionally protected when they tell students that there are a variety of ways to approach a given subject (Whitehead, 1994). John Whitehead points out that Supreme Court Justice Potter Stewart has specifically said that states may not punish teachers for telling students about the existence of other systems of respected human thought. Furthermore, a teacher who has a religious objection to teaching a particular piece of the curriculum should be accommodated by the school. Unfortunately, the courts are divided on this last point, particularly as it relates to the teaching of evolution. Because most courts hold that evolution is not a religious belief, many high school teachers have been contractually required to teach evolution.

May students read the Bible silently in the classroom?

Yes, if it is a free reading period and the teacher has allowed students to select their own reading material.

May students use faith-based topics in their work?

Yes, but they must follow the rules of the class. One area that has received a great deal of media attention is the debate about whether God is a person. When a teacher assigns students an essay on a person who has influenced them, some students will choose to write about God, Jesus, or another religious figure. In order to avoid controversy, teachers should be specific about the parameters of allowed topics.

How may I teach about religion in my class?

The NSBA has said that not only may you teach about religion in your class, but that education without "appropriate attention to major religious influences and themes is incomplete education" (*Religion, Education and the U.S. Constitution,* 1994, p. 163). The NSBA asserts that the study of religion can be integrated into existing courses that deal with history, society, family life, and community life, and that it can also be taught in special courses devoted to a comparative examination of world religions or religious literature. The board laments the fact that high school textbooks include little or nothing about the "great colonial revivals, the struggles of minority faiths, the religious motivations of immigrants, the contribution of religious groups to many social movements, major episodes of religious intolerance and other significant events of history" (p. 163).

Because religion plays a significant role in history and society, study about religion is essential to understanding both the nation and the world. Omission of facts about religion can give students the false impression that the religious life of humankind is insignificant or unimportant. Failure to understand even the basic symbols, practices, and concepts of the various religions makes much of history, literature, art, and contemporary life unintelligible. (p. 163)

However, if teachers are going to teach about religion, they must present the material in an "objective" format. There is a difference between teaching about religion and religious indoctrination. The NSBA and Haynes concur on the following guidelines:

The school's approach to religion should be *academic* not devotional.

The school may strive for student *awareness* of religions but should not press for student *acceptance* of any one religion.

The school may sponsor *study* about religion but may not sponsor the *practice* of religion.

The school may *expose* students to a diversity of religious views but may not *impose* any particular view.

The school may *educate* about all religions but may not *promote* or *denigrate* any religion.

The school may *inform* students about various beliefs but should not seek to *conform* them to any particular belief. (*Religion, Education and the U.S. Constitution*, 1994)

What is the difference between teaching values and teaching religion?

The NSBA says that teaching about religion is objective, academic study, while teaching values involves advocating particular ethical perspectives. The board specifically says that schools may teach about various religious and nonreligious moral perspectives on complex issues facing society, but teachers may not present these perspectives in ways that sponsor or denigrate one view over another. On the other hand, "basic moral values" that are recognized by all Americans, such as honesty, integrity, justice, and compassion, may be taught in classes through discussion and by example.

What is the difference between "basic moral values," other moral values, and religion?

These distinctions require a chapter of their own and will be addressed in chapter six.

It isn't always easy to know exactly what the law allows or requires with respect to religious freedom protection. However, there are a number of useful resources that can help teachers and administrators develop policies that are sensitive to the faith commitments of all students. Several of these organizations are listed in appendix A. Both the NSBA and the Freedom Forum regularly publish materials to help teachers understand their rights and obligations under the First Amendment.

6 Traditional Faith and the Secular Humanism Debate

Issues involving curriculum are sensitive because they hit at the tension between parents' desire to be the primary influence on their children and the government's desire to produce responsible citizens. Throughout the 1960s and 1970s, the Supreme Court heard a series of school cases that, while they served to secure for parents the right to educate children as they saw fit, also firmly emphasized that the state school system needs to be devoid of religious activity and the promotion of religious interests in order to maintain religious neutrality.

At the same time, however, the public school systems throughout the country were coming to grips with the fact that families could no longer be depended on to provide the moral foundation necessary for students to become fully responsible citizens. In the 1970s, "values clarification" courses were introduced in the public schools as a response to what some perceived as a gap in students' ethical development. Today, courses that encourage critical thinking by means of traditional liberal arts subject matters such as history are popular; critical thinking curriculum also molds high school units on sexuality and civics. For First Amendment purposes, the question is this: Can courses emphasizing values or morality be taught in a religiously neutral manner? The answer depends on the definition of *religious*.

This chapter examines federal court decisions concerning curriculum to uncover the judicial definition of *religion* as it affects public schools. Most of the cases have developed from a debate between the religious right and people who believe that "nonreligious" is the same as "religiously neutral." The argument of those who identify themselves as religious is twofold. Initially, parents claimed that if a school takes God out of the classroom, it is hostile toward religion, and this violates a child's Free Exercise rights. This perspective, for some, then developed into an Establishment Clause argument: You do not have to teach about God or Christian moral absolutes in the public school, but then you must also refrain from teaching moral absolutes of any other belief system—in fact, even moral relativism violates the Establishment Clause.

These arguments require analysis of the character and definition of *religion*. Judges face these arguments with trepidation, preferring to decide cases on any ground other than that of definition. But when the debate centers on the religious nature of beliefs such as scientific creationism, evolution, and secular humanism, the political climate in some states has forced judges to confront these questions head on. The political climate also forces teachers and administrators to enter the debate about religious versus ethical or moral curriculum. As difficult to follow as the litigation stories in this chapter may be, it is important for Christians to be grounded in the philosophical background of the debates. When teachers understand the foundations of the arguments, they can help parents and communities work through their differences and solve difficult curricular issues.

The Creation-Evolution Debate

Throughout the nineteenth and early twentieth centuries, many state school systems refused to teach evolution. In fact, numerous states made it a crime for teachers to introduce Darwinism to students. Science, particularly the study of the beginning of humanity, was based on Judeo-Christian precepts that included some concept of creation.

However, as the study of evolutionary process became more sophisticated and more accepted by scientists, some schools introduced evolution into their curriculum, often in violation of the law. The ensuing conflict developed into litigation that eventually reached the Supreme Court. In the 1920s, several southern states adopted the "monkey laws," which prohibited the teaching of the theory that people evolved from other species of life. From 1927 until the early 1960s, the public high schools of Arkansas complied with the law. In 1964, however, Susan Epperson, a high school teacher, was given a biology textbook for use in the coming school year. The textbook contained references to Darwinism. Epperson petitioned the state court for a declaration stating that the state statute criminalizing her use of the textbook violated the Establishment Clause of the First Amendment. The state courts of Arkansas refused to void the statute, but the case was appealed to the U.S. Supreme Court (*Epperson v. Arkansas,* 1968). The Supreme Court held that because the statute's purpose was to "blot out" theories that conflicted with the Bible, its purpose was religious not secular. Therefore, because the statue violated one of the prongs of the Lemon test (see chap. 4), the statute was void.

In response, the state passed a law stating that if schools were going to teach courses that referred to the origin of humanity, they had to use a balanced approach. If evolution was taught by teachers like Susan Epperson, then, in the name of religious and academic freedom, alternative views such as scientific creationism must also be presented. The federal court found this statute to be unconstitutional because it, too, failed the Lemon test; it had no secular purpose. This perspective was affirmed by the U.S. Supreme Court a few years later.

In *Edwards v. Aguillard* (1987), a case coming out of the state of Louisiana, the lower court had found that whether or not creation science was supported by scientific evidence, it was a religious belief. The case then turned on the purpose of the Louisiana Balanced Treatment Act, which had required state schools to teach creation if they also taught evolution. The court found that the act violated the First Amendment because it had no secular purpose. The belief it protected was religious, so the act had a religious purpose. On appeal, the state legislature pointed out that it had gone to great lengths to establish its secular purpose, the academic freedom of students, but the Supreme Court found this to be untrue and sustained the lower federal court's summary judgment overturning the state statute.

What Is the Issue?

The Supreme Court has held that the government may not establish a religion, nor may it establish a religion of secularism. However, the meaning of this directive is not clear unless *religion* and *secularism* are defined. In many cases, courts indicate that secularism exists when hostility to religion is exhibited. In curriculum cases, however, another approach comes to light. Some litigants do argue that schools violate their First Amendment religious freedom rights when books or curriculum present ideas that conflict with their religious beliefs. But other litigants take the argument in a different direction. They say that secularism itself is a faith. As such, if it is part of a curriculum in a public school, it violates the First Amendment. The first argument is based on the Free Exercise Clause, the second on the Establishment Clause.

The arguments can be demonstrated by examining the following statements:

1. Salvation comes from Mohammed not Jesus.
2. There is no such thing as salvation.
3. I'm okay; you're okay. Only you can determine what is right and what is wrong.

Which of these statements, if presented in a public school, attempts to establish a religion?

In order to answer that question, we must examine the two approaches the Supreme Court has taken regarding the definition of *religion*. In 1890, the Court said that religion was involved when one made reference to God or a deity (*Davis v. Beason*, 1890). This is referred to as the Davis definition of religion. But in 1967, the Court held that atheists were allowed to claim the religious conscientious objector status under federal law. The Court decided to allow this because it found that atheism reflected an "ultimate commitment." This "ultimate commitment" *functioned* as a religion (*United States v. Seeger*, 1965). The view that religion is not just belief in God but any ultimate commitment is referred to as the Seeger definition of religion. Based on these cases, the first statement above is clearly a religious statement and cannot be part of a school's curriculum. The second statement is hostile to religion, and many judges would find it also a violation of the First Amendment. But is the third statement religious? Is it nonreligious because it does not mention God, salvation, sin, prayer, or other concepts traditionally associated with formal religion (the Davis definition)? Or using the

Seeger definition of religion, does it reflect an ultimate value about humanity that functions as a faith commitment? The difference is important because it forms the foundation of the debates that make up modern-day curriculum wars. In the creation science cases throughout the 1970s, federal courts took their cue from *Epperson,* striking down a variety of state methods that tried to force inclusion of alternative explanations of life when evolution was taught. Because the judges in the *Epperson* case had focused on the *purpose* of the statute, the claim that both evolution and creation science were based on belief systems received little analysis. However, although the nature of religion was not specifically addressed, judges were hard pressed to avoid the argument that students were indeed being indoctrinated into one particular way of thinking. Some courts acknowledged this; others did not.

In *Wright v. Houston* (1972), a federal court dismissed a case in which parents sought to enjoin a school district from teaching evolution exclusively and uncritically. In arguing for balanced treatment of creation science, the parents presented two arguments. First, evolution contradicted their religious beliefs. The school's role in discouraging students' belief in creation was a restraint on the free exercise of religion for those students. Second, evolution was part of a religion of secularism. Thus, if taught in public schools, it was establishment of religion. The court refused to accept either argument, saying that, obviously, there was no connection between evolution and religion. The interesting thing, though, is that the court used the definition of *religion* presented by the Supreme Court in the 1890 *Davis* case. Religion means relationship to a creator. Evolution does not mention a creator; thus, evolution is not a religion.

Despite the reference to an old Supreme Court definition of *religion,* the court's decision seems to have been molded mainly by pragmatic problems. The judge was particularly troubled by the practical ramifications of deciding in any other way. He said that although the equal time approach advocated by the plaintiffs did seem fair,

> virtually every religion known to man holds its own peculiar view of human origins. Within the scientific community itself, there is much debate over the details of the theory of evolution. This Court is hardly qualified to select from among the available theories those which merit attention in a public school biology class. (*Wright v. Houston,* 1972, p. 1211)

But to the litigants, this was exactly the point. There is debate about the origin of man. And one's point of view about the origin of man depends on what one holds to be ultimately true. According to the *Seeger* case, this ultimate truth is religion. Even in the scientific community there is no cohesive body of knowledge regarding how man came to be that all scientists accept as fact. Evolutionists must accept some "facts" on faith (Johnson, 1993). So if one perspective is taught to the exclusion of others, are children receiving "neutral" education? Is the perspective they are taught devoid of religion if one uses the Seeger definition of *religion* rather than the Davis definition? No doubt it would be onerous for the public school system to teach all alternative views of the origin of man, but this difficulty does not change the fact that evolution is based on fundamental assumptions about the world that must be accepted on faith, just as is creation science.

Secular Humanism as a Religion

The argument that evolution is based on a theory of life that is foundational, or religious, has not been persuasive to judges. However, soon after the deluge of creation-science cases swept the federal courts, the interest of some judges was piqued by the argument that religion did not necessarily mean "relating to God." Although evolution may not be religion, there could still be other types of curriculum approaches that did reflect religious commitment. Two lines of federal court cases explored this concept throughout the 1980s. Although appellate courts in each line of cases ultimately found that secular humanism was not a religion, the careful analysis that some of the judges went through to define *religion* and *religious belief* is instructive, and it may influence religious freedom cases in the future.

The Holt Basic Readings Cases

In 1984, a group of children and their parents brought suit against a Tennessee school district, claiming that the textbooks used to teach reading to elementary school students violated the free exercise rights of Christian students. The claim was that the Holt Basic Readings series did the following:

1. taught witchcraft and other forms of magic and occult activity
2. taught that values are relative
3. taught disrespect and disobedience to parents
4. depicted prayer to idols
5. taught that faith in the supernatural was acceptable for salvation
6. depicted children who were disrespectful during Bible study
7. implied that Jesus was illiterate
8. taught that people and apes had common ancestors
9. taught humanistic values

Initially, the court found against the parents, saying that the First Amendment did not protect the plaintiffs from mere exposure to offensive value systems or antithetical religious ideas.

Only if the plaintiffs can prove that the books at issue are teaching a particular religious faith as true (rather than as a cultural phenomenon), or teaching that the students must be saved through some religious pathway, or that no salvation is required, can it be said the mere exposure to these books is a violation of free exercise rights. (*Mozert v. Hawkins,* 1984, p. 1053)

All counts except number five were thrown out of the case. Then the court decided the case should be dismissed as to count number five also, because the poems and stories that the plaintiffs objected to met the court's Lemon test of neutrality. The Holt Basic Readings neither advocated a particular religious belief nor expressed hostility to religion. Although the stories, which included Hindu fables and Anne Frank's discussion of religion as a belief in "something," did discuss religion, they did not tell the students to believe particular things.

The plaintiffs correctly reach the obvious conclusion that this poem [the Hindu elephant fable stating as its moral that in theology disputants are often partly right and wrong] meant that each religion described God from its own limited vantage point, based on its incomplete revelation, and that all are only partly right and partly wrong. While that is no doubt the meaning of the poem, there is nothing in the book to suggest that all should subscribe to this way of thinking. The poem is presented for what it is worth. *In the context of the readers taken as a whole, however, it does indeed illustrate the type of religious tolerance presumably requisite to the ideal "world citizen."* (*Mozert v. Hawkins,* p. 202, emphasis added)

Here the court's vision of neutrality is clear. Value neutrality occurs when religious belief is not advocated, nor is hostility presented. The school superintendent defended his decision to use the Holt books on the ground that they enhanced reading skills. No proselytizing occurred.

The appellate court overturned the lower court's summary judgment saying that the lower court should have had a trial based on this question: Did the school district *try* to accommodate the free exercise rights of the children? If not, the "least restrictive alternative" prong of the strict scrutiny test (chap. 4) was probably violated.

The problem, however, was both courts missed the point of the plaintiffs' arguments. The plaintiffs stated that not only was the reading material hostile to their religious belief (a free exercise issue) but that the school was teaching an alternative belief system (an establishment issue). Neutrality toward religion does not come about merely by eliminating negative connotations of religion; neutrality requires recognition of the fact that any teaching of ethical values stems from a foundational commitment that parallels a religious commitment. Religion involves salvation and prayer and ritual, certainly, but it is also an ethical system, and alternative ethical systems are not neutral; they *replace* Christianity. As such, they constitute establishment of religion just as much as the teaching of creationism or biblical mandates.

The judges analyzing the Holt Basic Readings series did not provide an answer to this argument. However, at the same time these cases were taking place, Judge William Brevard Hand in Alabama decided that the parallel between secular humanism and theistic religion deserved serious judicial attention.

The Jaffree and Smith Cases

In May 1982, Ishmael Jaffree sued the Mobile Alabama County School Board, seeking a judgment declaring prayer activities in the public school system to be violative of the First Amendment. Douglas Smith and others intervened in the Jaffree suit, claiming that if prayer were eliminated, their religious free exercise rights would be violated. In addition, they claimed that if an injunction were set forth against the Christian activities in the schools, then an injunction should also be imposed against the religions of secularism, humanism, evolution, materialism, agnosticism, and atheism. This complicated case was bifurcated into a school prayer argument, which was taken up first, and a curriculum argument, which never reached the Supreme Court. On the issue of prayer in school, the Supreme Court upheld the circuit court's decision, finding that prayer violated the Establishment Clause. The vigor of the litigation, however, and the vehemence of Justice William Rehnquist's dissent shed light on several aspects of the definition of *religion* and *neutrality toward religion.*

Initially, the district court had found that the Supreme Court had erred in its earlier decisions that applied the Establishment Clause to state governments. At the time the First Amendment was ratified, many states had established state churches. Judge Hand found that historical evidence made it clear that the framers of the Constitution intended the Establishment Clause of the First Amendment to apply only to the establishment of a *national* church. Therefore, in keeping with the doctrine of original intent for constitutional interpretation, state institutions such as schools should be allowed to establish religion.

Hand anticipated that his decision would be overturned, so he took the opportunity to caution the judges who examined his decision to think carefully about the nature of faith commitments. He stated:

> Case law deals generally with removing the teachings of the Christian ethic from the scholastic effort but totally ignores the teaching of the secular humanist ethic. It was pointed out in the testimony that the curriculum in the public schools of Mobile County is rife with efforts at teaching or encouraging secular humanism—all without opposition from any other ethic—to such an extent that it becomes a brain-

washing effort. If this Court is compelled to purge "God is great, God is good, we thank Him for our daily food" from the classroom, *then this Court must also purge from the classroom those things that serve to teach that salvation is through one's self rather than through a deity.* (*Jaffree v. Board of School Comm'rs,* 1983, p. 1129, emphasis added)

Hand's decision in the *Jaffree* case was successfully appealed on the issue of school prayer when the circuit court and the Supreme Court both ignored Hand's historical perspective. Both the circuit court and the Supreme Court used the *Lemon* case to hold that prayer violated the Establishment Clause because it fostered religion. Then a new line of cases began on the curriculum issue (referred to as the Smith cases). Hand's decision in *Jaffree* laid the groundwork for his careful and lengthy analysis of the nature of religion in the *Smith* case (*Smith v. Board of School Comm'rs,* 1987).

In the *Smith* case, Judge Hand had to determine whether secular humanism was a religion and, if so, whether it was established in the public school through the use of certain textbooks.

The plaintiffs said that secular humanism existed in the schools in the following manner:

God was left out of all discussions of the origin of the universe and all discussions of right and wrong.

Teachers and students were required to use books that took the Lord's name in vain.

Students were encouraged to question the authority of parents, and "people in charge" were depicted as those who would use students for their own personal gain.

Students were taught that there were no moral absolutes and that humans were merely a result of a biological process.

The school district defended its approach, saying it was religiously neutral in that it was not hostile toward religion. The district claimed secular humanism is not a religion, and even if it is, it is established by the Constitution. The two sides were not merely at cross-purposes, they were coming at the issue of religious neutrality from different perspectives. One argued that religious neutrality occurs when hostility is eliminated; the other argued that neutrality cannot occur until it is recognized that all ethical systems are based in religion of one type or another. These perspectives on religious neutrality stemmed from different definitions of *religion*. If religion is purely private faith in God and does not necessarily have implications for all of life, then employment and schooling can be done in a religiously neutral manner as long as God is kept out of them. If, however, one has an integrated view of life, if one believes all decisions in life including employment and schooling issues stem from a foundational belief system, then keeping God out of these decisions rejects theistic religion, but it does not escape being "religious" in a broad sense of the word.

Professor Richard Baer, one of the witnesses in the *Smith* case, explains:

It is incorrect to assume that one can divide the world neatly into the realm of the religious and the realm of the nonreligious or secular. In a narrow sense of the term religious, this is possible. It is not difficult, for instance, to distinguish between a baptismal service or a bar mitzvah as cultic practices on the one hand and the secular activities of repairing a washing machine or teaching mathematics. But many theologians and sociologists argue that in a broader sense religion is that dimension of human culture (along with metaphysics) which is concerned about questions of the meaning of life and humanity's place in the universe. In this sense Marxist philosophy and other specially secular and humanistic philosophies speak to questions that are religious. I do not mean by this the patronizing view that even atheists secretly believe in God. There are bona fide atheists just as there are bonafide theists. Rather, I refer to the fact that human beings live out their lives in relation to certain basic values that provide meaning and purpose to life. These values function in the life of the atheist in a way that is functionally similar to the way belief in God functions in the life of the theist. (Baer, 1987, p. 5–6)

Judge Hand seemed to recognize this problem. In his decision, he took testimony from groups of experts to determine answers to the following questions:

What is the nature of education and the learning process?
What is a religion?
Is secular humanism a religion?
Is secular humanism exhibited in the public schools?

Hand was persuaded by witnesses for both the plaintiffs and the defendants that schooling in the United States involves much more than the mere transmittal of information to students. Teachers and education psychology experts testified that schools are concerned with interpreting facts for students, going so far as to say that the purpose of a school is to develop citizens for a "just world, to develop a humane being." Teachers and textbooks are a significant part of this development; therefore, the testimony of people who deciphered the philosophies outlined in the texts became important to Hand. If the philosophies were religious, they violated the First Amendment. Hand, unlike other judges, recognized that before he could address this question, he had to come to grips with a working definition of *religious*.

Referring to the Seeger definition of religion, Hand found that under the First Amendment, government may not define religion by reference to the validity of the beliefs or practices involved. Content-based definitions result in showing favoritism to some religions. Rather,

> the state must instead look to *factors common to all religious* movements to decide how to distinguish those ideologies worthy of the protection of the religion clauses from those which must seek refuge under other constitutional provision. (*Smith v. Board of School Comm'rs,* 655 7. Supp. 939, 1987, p. 978, emphasis added)

Only after one has done this can one distinguish between people's right to define their religious belief and government's right to regulate activities to protect other rights and privileges that are "unrelated to religion." In a footnote, Hand qualified this phrase by saying that if some faiths do not separate actions that are determined by faith and actions that are "unrelated" to religion, government still has the right to supersede religious freedom in order to protect the things that are necessary to have religious freedom: "life, an orderly civilization, peace, protection of the material means for preserving life" (p. 979).

Hand then defined *religion* as systems of belief that encompass "fundamental assumptions" about such things as the existence of transcendent reality, the nature of man or the goal of man's existence, and the purpose and nature of the universe. He said that in some belief systems these assumptions are less explicit than in others, but it is important to realize that what often masquerades as "neutral" thought is, in fact, based in foundational belief. This foundational belief is the functional equivalent of religion.

> Whenever a belief system deals with fundamental questions of the nature of reality and man's relationship to reality, *it deals with essentially religious questions.* A religion need not posit a belief in a deity, or a belief in supernatural existence. A religious person adheres to some position on whether su-

pernatural and/or transcendent reality exists at all, and if so, how, and if not, why. (p. 979, emphasis added)

But only belief that addresses these ultimate values should be protected by the First Amendment.

A mere "comprehensive world-view" or "way of life" is not by itself enough to identify a belief system as religious. A world-view may be merely economic, or sociological, and a person might choose to follow a "way of life" that ignores ultimate issues addressed by religions. Describing a belief as comprehensive is too vague to be an effective definition under the religion clauses: some religious persons may consider some issues as peripheral that others find central to their beliefs. Diet is one example of this. Another is the devotion of some religions to a non-technological life-style, such as the Amish. A person can be religious for first amendment purposes without having rules and regulations governing every aspect of every day conduct. Equating comprehensiveness with religion results in an overinclusive definition. (p. 979)

Using this definition of *religion*, Christianity is a religion. But to Hand, so is secular humanism. Experts at the trial defined secular humanism as:

a creed or world view which holds that we have no reason to believe in a creator, that the world is self existing, that there is no transcendent power at work in the world, that we should not turn to traditional religion for wisdom; rather that we should develop a new ethics [sic] and a new method of moral order founded upon the teachings of modern naturalism and physical science. (p. 986)

The experts explained that secular humanists are not pious, do not believe in transcendent beings, and do not pray. The belief system is not a dogma or a doctrine, but it does express moral values.

Based on the testimony, Hand found that secular humanism makes statements about the existence of supernatural existence, sets goals for human existence, and defines the nature of the universe. The substance of the belief system is that all of reality can be known by the human intellect "aided only by the devices of man's creation or discovery. . . . By the force of logic, the universe is self-existing, knowable. . . . Moreover, man is the product of biology with no spiritual dimension" (p. 985).

When Hand applied his definition of *religion* to the perspective of the textbooks, he found that the books did establish humanism. The home economics textbooks used by the students required them to accept as true the fact that people use the same process in deciding a moral issue that they use in "choosing one pair of shoes over another" and that "the student must determine right and wrong based only on his own experience, feelings and [internal] values" (p. 986).

In support of his finding, Hand gave several examples. The home economics textbook *Teen Guide* stated: "Nothing was meant to be. You are the designer of your life. If you want something, you can plan and work for it. Nothing is easy, but nothing is impossible, either. When you recognize that you are the one in charge of your life, you will be way ahead of where you would be if you think of your life as something that just happens to you" (p. 973). Hand pointed out that this encouraged students to believe that only they could decide what is right and wrong.

It is to be contrasted to telling a student that he is responsible for choosing between right and wrong. The latter promotes responsibility. . . . The point made is that such teaching leaves out the distinction that must be drawn between what moral values are to be freely chosen and the personal decision involved in applying these values. (p. 973)

Furthermore, another book stated that although six- and seven-year-olds are content to be their mother's daughter or their father's son, older children probably do not feel this way. "In adolescence people begin defining the world for themselves in their own way. They no longer want to be just someone's son or daughter. They want to be a unique person. They want to discover life and themselves on their own" (p. 974).

Judge Hand accepted the testimony of witnesses who explained that this perspective was evidence of a belief system that taught human responsibility is self-directed. This competed with belief systems that teach there is a divine source for determining the way life ought to be lived.

When texts taught students that they could prepare themselves to make the "right decisions" by working on their self-concept and accepting themselves and believing in themselves, students were indoctrinated into "individualism" to the exclusion of other belief systems. The argument that validity of moral choice is determined by the individual is not religiously neutral. Not only does it undermine traditional religious faiths, but it, itself, is a belief system that competes with faith.

According to Hand, "The emphasis and overall approach [of the books implies] and would cause any reasonable thinking student to infer, that the book[s are] teaching that moral choices are just a matter of preferences, because, as the books say 'you are the most important person in your life'" (p. 986). Issues of moral choice stem from a person's view of man and humanity's place in the universe. They are solved by belief systems. If schools teach that these choices are to be solved in an individualistic manner, this is a functional substitute for saying that moral choice ought to be solved by reference to the Bible.

Hand stated that

the highly relativistic and individualistic approach constitutes the promotion of a fundamental faith claim [and] assumes that self-actualization is the goal of every human being, that man has no supernatural attributes or component, that there are only temporal and physical consequences for man's action, and that these results, alone, determine the morality of an action. [This belief] strikes at the heart of many theistic religions' beliefs that certain actions are in and of themselves immoral, whatever the consequences, and that, in addition, actions will have extratemporal consequences. (p. 986–87)

Therefore, it is hostile to many religions. "Some religious beliefs are so fundamental that the act of denying them will completely undermine that religion" (p. 987). But, more importantly, "denial of that belief will result in the affirmance of a contrary belief and result in the establishment of an opposing religion" (p. 987). While the state may teach certain moral values, such as lying is wrong, "if, in so doing it advances a reason for the rule, the possible different reasons must be explained evenhandedly" and "the state may not promote one particular reason over another in the public schools" (p. 988).

On appeal, the circuit court treated Hand's analysis with the same summary dismissal that it employed when it ignored his examination of constitutional history in the *Jaffree* case. The appellate court held that even if secular humanism were a religion, the mere presentation of religious belief did not constitute establishment of religion. Moreover, the books were used to promote critical thinking, independent thought, tolerance of diverse views, self-respect, and maturity. Furthermore, the court said, one of the major objectives of public education is to inculcate fundamental values necessary to maintain democracy. This was all, obviously, "an entirely appropriate secular effect" (*Smith v. Board of Comm'rs,* 827 F.2d, p. 692). This court clearly missed the point of the lower court's discussion when it stated the following:

> The public schools in this country are organized on the premise that secular education can be isolated from all religious teaching so that the school can inculcate all needed temporal knowledge and also maintain a strict and lofty neutrality as to religion. The assumption is that after the individual has been instructed in worldly wisdom he will be better fitted to choose his religion. (p. 695)

The Issue of Neutrality

Judge Hand's recognition of secular humanism as a religion seems to be based on his belief that much of the knowledge transmitted in the schools is of social construction. Steven Tipton writes that the meaning of "mutuality, civil spirit, and justice," or the content of our values, are not uniformly self-evident to everyone. This is because our interests conflict, certainly. But, he explains, it is also because everyone construes meaning within different cultural and moral conditions. Value neutrality does not exist because people are not objective. Our meaning is determined by our experience and our belief.

Even if you say that you want to achieve value neutrality by even handedly presenting all points of view, you miss the point. The whole concept of value neutrality is, itself, biased towards value systems that are tolerant or based on consensual arrangement. Law professor Stanley Ingber points out that value neutrality

> posits individual criticism and moral choice as values unto themselves. Consequently, a "value-neutral" education would oppose perspectives, such as fundamental Christianity, that advocates imposing values. (Ingber, 1989, p. 239)

Moreover, even though value neutrality or ethical subjectivism sound like the kind of tolerance schools in democratic society should foster, they contradict themselves.

Richard Baer has written that these systems claim they tell no one what is good or right for them. He says that we act as if people can choose their own values.

> But this is misleading. To be specific, if all values are subjective, matters of personal feeling, then we can place no absolute values on things as justice, tolerance of people who hold dissenting views, freedom and equality, or even democracy itself. (Baer, 1987, p. 15)

The fact is most Americans do believe that values rest on some foundation greater than simple consensus. Some things are fundamentally true and good; we possess certain inalienable rights in addition to whatever those in power might believe or however they might act at any given point in time (Ingber, 1989). What is this foundational truth other than an equivalent to the moral foundation of Christianity, Judaism, or Buddhism? As Baer suggests, moral values come from a worldview.

The problem is that when a state school tries to teach students how they should act, the "should" will always come from some fundamental perspective of what humanity ought to be. This is at the root of curricular disputes. And you cannot solve curricular disputes if you do not understand the faith commitments of all parties involved. People in this country disagree about the nature of religious belief, they disagree about the difference between morals and faith, and they disagree about the role that faith plays in determining "meaning."

Because so much disagreement exists concerning these issues, it is extremely important to keep in mind the guidelines suggested by Charles Haynes discussed in chapter 5. Schools are to be a market place of ideas; when curricular conflicts arise we should start at the point of agreement, and we should make sure the school clearly communicates its policies to everyone.

7 A Cloud of Witnesses

All across North America, Christians are teaching in public schools. In this chapter, these teachers speak for themselves. You will notice that out of their zeal or due to lack of information concerning the law, some of these teachers are saying or doing things in the classroom that are not within the boundaries of what the law allows. Others are struggling to teach in ways that are within the legal guidelines but that are also in keeping with their religious beliefs. All of them, however, give clear witness to the fact that they know they are called to serve in this part of the kingdom of God.

The following responses, taken from our interviews with many groups of teachers, were organized according to topic. The names of the teachers have been changed in order to protect their schools and positions.

Why is it important for Christians to teach in public schools?

Greg: It's the same reason that Christians should be in every walk of life. We speak from a variety of denominational backgrounds around this table. In my denomination we believe that we are all ministers, not all clergy but all ministers in whatever we do. I believe that the most important job there is is teaching, and therefore, we need to bring our faith to that. I'm not talking about the Pharisee standing on the corner, but just being there every day, with the idea that Christ is there with you. It means doing the type of things that say, "My faith is in Christ and because of that, through the Spirit, things happen that we don't even know." It has to do with caring and listening.

Cindy: I believe that if we walk our talk the kids will see there is something different about us. We don't heckle other teachers or talk about the kids negatively. The kids can feel safe with us. And if they challenge me they find out they can ask me questions, and, even though they don't believe what I believe, we can talk about it. It's about standing for what you believe. It is in the way you deal with kids. They know you won't jump all over them. They can see that something is different.

Marta: I try to get out of my head the idea of how a child should be; I try to look at how the child actually is. That tells me that instead of saying, "This child should be able to sit in this reading group and behave in this way," I need to say, "What should I do to help this child learn?" And that's a real struggle because my mind-set is so middle class and I have the idea that students should be able to come to school ready to learn, but often they're not. I think my faith speaks to that in my classroom as much as anything else—learning to ask who or what do I need to become in order to help this child learn because that is the job God has given me to do. And in respect for this child I must stop thinking about the imperfections and look at what the strengths are.

Interviewer: It is interesting to hear you say that, because I think some Christians have in mind how a person ought to act, and then if he or she acts differently, that person is wrong.

Marta: Yes, of course there are some standards. A child may not hurt another child, for example. But for learning I believe it is my responsibility to figure out who the child is and not who the child should be.

Sarah: So you're saying, "Don't blame the child if he is not able to learn. Just take control for what you can do, and for you that is part of being a Christian."

Marta: Yes, and try to be less judgmental.

How does a teacher's Christian worldview affect the teaching task?

Jack: Basically, as a Christian, I think of becoming more knowledgeable as to what that means. I know that over the years I have tried to exhibit more fruit of the Spirit, particularly in areas such as patience and kindness toward the kids, whereas before I probably would not have looked at it quite that way.

Also, I try to avoid situationalism, meaning simply that in our environment if children are misbehaving or not producing we often look at the home. The administration pushes this. "They're from a poor home environment," or "They're having a bad day," as if that is a justification for poor behavior. That might be a reason for poor behavior, but that doesn't make poor behavior right, and I try to look at it in that way.

I try to look at the idea that we're training up children, just as parents should be training up children, according to what it says in Proverbs. So I try to look at it from a positive perspective. I'm not going to work to get a paycheck, although that's part of it, but certainly when I'm looking at the children this is what I'm supposed to be doing—taking an active role in training them.

Suzanne: The fact that I teach in the Bible Belt has everything to do with the fact that my students even know about Christ's death on the cross. Flannery O'Connor wrote, "I think it is safe to say that, while the South is hardly Christ-centered, it is most certainly Christ-haunted." A few hundred yards from my school there is an olive canvas tent that is the headquarters for the Last Call Revival, and "getting saved" is a monthly ritual for a few of my students. In other words, they have the vocabulary for these discussions, but the theology can be pretty twisted.

Interviewer: Would you say that most of your students are Christians?

Suzanne: While most of my students would describe themselves as "Christian," few of them seem to have a real understanding of what that means in terms of a life of discipleship. Getting sprinkled, poured, or dunked is what it's about for most of them, and then they go blithely on. As one of my students airily told me when I questioned something he had said about his lifestyle that seemed in direct contradiction to his Christian profession, "Oh, God understands." For those students who are self-proclaimed Christians, I view it as part of my responsibility as an educator to educate them about the faith they profess. If one of them described himself or herself as a Democrat or Republican, I would certainly want to help them clarify what that meant, what the traditional platform and foundational perspectives of the Democratic or Republican party are, so I think it is perfectly appropriate to help students understand more clearly what it means to be a Christian if that's what they are calling themselves. I do refer to the Bible in such discussions by saying, "Well, this is what the Bible says about that . . ." and I view this, again, as clarifying—educating—rather than proselytizing.

Joel: I've taken a view that we're supposed to be salt and light and we're supposed to, when opportunities present themselves, be a witness for Christ. Maybe not necessarily always verbal, but the way we behave, the way we respond, whether we're patient, whether we care about the students.

One of the things I've always tried to do is really not look at the subject matter I'm teaching as the most important thing, but that the students are the most important thing. If they're learning to enjoy what I teach, they'll learn, but they can also learn some lessons about getting along with other people, and giving their best effort, and things like that. I really do look at it like we're also there to give them some values, whether they're the values we teach them or the values we model.

Betty: I have my class list and I've already started praying for next year's kids. Where my Christian faith has made all the difference is that I really love the kids, and I try to see them as a whole. I originally taught at a school where the kids were really needy—needed clothes, supplies, all kinds of things. I think when you love students and you see them as a whole, you try to jump in to help with all their needs.

It's very important to know their strengths and to know their weaknesses so you can help them with their weaknesses and help them play to their strengths. But as has been said, patience, kindness, and all the fruits of the Spirit are things that I try very purposefully to pray for and to work on, to help them be the very best that they can be.

I try to think of my classroom as a family, a home away from home, and I try to meet all kinds of needs. I have kids who are a source of irritation, and we just didn't hit it off. I always say, "Lord, give me one thing about them that I can really love," and I try to go on that. I have had students I did not like, and I asked the Lord to show me one thing to really play up, and you know what happened? Just like C. S. Lewis said, don't worry spending time saying, "Do I love this person; do I not love that person?" He said just act as if you love them and you'll end up loving them, and that's really true.

Jack: To carry that a step further, I sometimes think about the fact that even if I don't love them, God loves them, and that helps me to see them as people of value and worth, even if I don't see anything of great value. In addition, I try to remember that they are their parents' most precious possessions, and I need to see them that way too and treat them as individuals. I've always seen myself foremost as a teacher. The subject matter is secondary to that because we're teaching in so many different areas of life and not just a particular academic subject.

Maxine: I think of seeing children as created in the image of God. There may be teachers who would appear to be more compassionate and more kind, but sometimes the best thing for someone is the hard thing. Real love will see to that rather than just allowing things to go on. Often I'll say to my kids, "Do you know why I want you to do this? Because I really care about what happens to you." And I hope that's reflected in my relationship with my kids.

Matthew: When we discuss a theory, I explain that there are different views held by scientists, and just because some or many scientists may believe one theory today, when they find new evidence they may change their minds. If I teach something contrary to Scripture, I always tell the other side. Evolution, for example. I warn kids that in high school and college they may be taught something that Jews, Muslims, or Christians don't believe, and even though their teacher may have all the answers, they should wait before they believe that teacher because other equally intelligent teachers may come along with different answers.

Priscilla: I try to make sure that the materials I teach with won't offend my students no matter what faith they are. I don't discuss or teach religion in the public school. I hope through my actions as a role model and through my happiness I can convey that I am a Christian. I don't believe I should push Christianity onto my students in a public school. I wouldn't want my kids learning to believe in Buddhism in a public school.

Angelica: The life witness in the classroom has got to be the most influential thing we can do, what the students observe. Students see this and begin to question what makes you different. So-and-so reacts differently when we do this, but you didn't. The happiness component certainly is there, but it is much more than that. It is life encompassing. There used to be a debate in my denomination concerning whether one could say, "By his life witness you would know him." The other side would say, "Well, my goodness that's not enough. That's even a cop-out." But the presence of a Christian teacher is a very powerful presence. You build a relationship. You treat a student in a certain way. You see value in that person and you treat that person as a person of value. That often becomes a defining moment when the student thinks, "Oh, she thinks there is something decent about me." And you become a stunningly important person in that student's life. Then their questions come from that. I was looking through my journal from earlier years in a former school. There's a whole page devoted to what I call "Questions from the Hood." A large percentage of them relate to spiritual matters such as, "Is my boyfriend who was shot in a drug deal watching me from heaven?" Well, the theological issues right there are overwhelming.

Interviewer: How did you answer that?

Angelica: She returned to class and had a kind of catharsis about this grief experience. Family members would say,

"Well, he's watching you." And I guess my first thought was, "I doubt he's watching you from there, but we don't have the whole story, do we?" I don't know. I think probably because it was a class situation I begged off the question and said, "Why do you think he is?" Which may be a cop-out, but I felt I couldn't really give her the assurance about him. I don't think she was so much looking for answers as looking for a place to talk about this.

They asked me once why things can't be perfect, and I answered by saying, "Well, there's a book that says things were perfect once. Some people believe it and some people don't. But that book, for whatever reason, says that things were perfect." "Well," they asked, "what happened?" That's probably as close as I came during class time to talking about the Bible. In that school there were many references to spiritual matters. I think it was because their lives were so impoverished, and they were truly looking for something. They were looking for order and answers and solutions to the chaos.

Greg: I have some of the same struggles, but one of the things I have come to understand through my own Bible reading is that I keep wanting to say, "Well, how am I going to be able to help them?" when, in actuality, if we look to the New Testament, God says, "Do your best and I'll let the Spirit work out the details." If instead of thinking of myself as the salve I look at myself as being the vessel that contains the salve, then God will do the work. I am better off then. The best thing we can do is sit there and listen. And we aren't too busy because we know that Christ listened.

Angelica: But then when you get into those gut-level issues, life issues, and they truly are looking for answers and you feel that you may go up to a certain point and may not go any further, it becomes a very difficult thing. You are withholding information that they could use. You really are not allowed to give it. What role then do you take? So you probably stay in the middle of the road with a little of this and a little of that without getting into trouble, but then after a while you get to feel sort of pharisaical about that because you aren't really handing out the major medicine. You're just kind of deflecting and trying to give them a decent answer. I remember one student coming to me after class saying, "You believe that God stuff, don't you?" I said, "Yes I do. Why do you ask?" He said, "I can tell." And he turned and left. But he had to know. He took the time to confront me. He wanted an answer and he got one. At what point do you get to be a Pharisee because you stop short?

Greg: Well, I don't have that because I don't stop short.

Angelica: So what would you do? Would you give them the message of salvation in class?

Greg: I think standing on the corner yelling the message at the top of your lungs is the cheap way. You're not investing your whole life into it. That's cheap. No, if people ask me I will give my opinion. I will not try to proselytize.

Cindy: Something we haven't touched on is the fact that being a Christian teacher in a public school strengthens other Christians. I'm amazed and encouraged by how many kids know so firmly what they believe. Nobody approached me when I was a student. I was taught right and wrong, but I had no idea there was something more back then. These kids need someone to identify with because they feel lonely, as if there's no one else out there.

Eric: They need this cloud of witnesses. A large part of what we call "Christian love" is to put yourself in someone else's place. It comes from the whole idea of God becoming man. As man, God can understand what we are going through. I think that is what Christian love is all about—putting yourself in another person's place. Asking, "What is that person going through?" rather than thinking that that person is making me uncomfortable.

Interviewer: You are talking about imaging God in the classroom.

Eric: Exactly. Being Christlike.

Interviewer: Do you think being a mature Christian gives you a kind of buffer so that what a student says doesn't have to hurt you so much?

Angelica: Perhaps. Not that it doesn't hurt you but that you don't move. You are experienced enough to absorb their behavior and still go on having a good relationship with the student. Being able to give a soft answer or an appropriate answer that allows the student to save face and to stay in the classroom and feel okay about himself. You are seasoned and can absorb it and let it go.

Cindy: Maybe maturity brings with it the ability to select the things you think really must be changed.

Eric: Exactly. Choose your battles.

Cindy: For me, learning more about what it means that I am a child of God is what really supports me when there are critics or when my advanced class of students all think they should be valedictorian or they don't like the way I grade. When I go home at night it still hurts, but I am able to think, "But God says that this is who I am and this is what is true." That has made a huge difference to me.

Angelica: Experience allows you not to have to defend yourself every time you perceive you've been attacked or every time you actually have been attacked. Sometimes it is only a perception.

Eric: As a teacher you're so vulnerable. You've got the kids and the parents. All these people make judgments about what you are doing. And maybe you've made a bad call. Sometimes you do.

Interviewer: You've been doing this for thirty years. Are kids much different now from fifteen years ago?

Eric: I love that question. My feeling about that is that I've changed so much. I don't really think they have changed. Fifteen-year-olds have always been fifteen-year-olds.

Angelica: That is a rare and gracious response. So many "lifers" say, "I can't stand these kids. I wish it were twenty years ago when kids were teachable." I've never heard someone who has been in it your length of time say, "Well, I've changed."

Eric: I don't know if they are more difficult to teach now. If you believe what the Bible says about the condition of man, you will realize that it has always been this way, always difficult. It just shows itself in different ways. I remember some very rowdy students my first year of teaching back in the sixties. I was so scared some days I didn't want to go to school. I wasn't afraid of the kids, but I was so unsure of what I was doing. I felt no support from the rest of the staff. The staff had doubled in size that year because of all the new students, and the older staff members stayed by themselves as if to say, "We're not going to help you guys."

Pope John XXIII said something that is good advice for teachers: "Be aware of everything, overlook a great deal, correct little." That's helped me in recent years. As a teacher you have to be aware of everything that is going on but you have to overlook a lot. You will be burned out if you try to stop everything that is wrong.

In your experience has a teacher ever gotten into trouble for being "too Christian"?

Eric: I guess I'm confused as to what the law says. I thought the law says that I can't preach in the sense that I'm telling somebody that the way I believe is the only correct way and that they will go to hell if they don't believe that. But if someone asks me if I go to church and what my church teaches, I always thought I could talk about that. A great many teachers are confused about what the law actually says. In speech and debate we get into this all the time. I had a class last semester in which I believe we talked about religion almost 90 percent of the time.

Angelica: Which is an indication that they are looking for something real, the genuine article.

Eric: The only problem I had was with a girl who was a fundamentalist Christian. She told people that if they don't believe exactly the way she believes, they will go to hell, especially the Roman Catholics.

Interviewer: She said that in class?

Eric: Most definitely in class, in almost every speech she gave. I tried to protect her as much as I could even though I didn't agree with her, but the other kids were really getting mad at her. Their parents were getting mad at her. I never got into trouble for it, but the other students' parents talked to the principal about it. I have kids talking about religion all the time. They ask my opinion and I give it. But I say that I am not telling them what they have to believe.

Tom: I think in the years I was principal only once did a problem arise. I had some very fundamentalistic, very evangelistic staff members, and they didn't always show great wisdom as to what was appropriate. I suppose they felt that because I was a Christian principal they had a certain freedom too. I tended to hear more about inappropriateness from other members of the staff rather than from students or parents. Generally, though, I think Christian teachers tend to be too careful. They could handle it better by being more open. One thing I learned about teenagers is that they like to be taken seriously, and they will take you seriously too. You will be able to get into some fundamental issues if you are showing your students respect.

Marvin: I can agree with that. There are so many opportunities to discuss your faith. The kids really want to know about you. Not just the guy in front of the class but what kind of person you are outside of the classroom. What do you do? Are you married? Do you have kids? Where do you go on your vacation? They want to know personal things about you. Not very important things, but they want to know who you are. What church do you go to? It happens that I have some friends at New Covenant Church. One of my boys came late to class and said, "I'm sorry I'm late. The youth pastor took me out to lunch." "Oh, yes, Les Wiseman. I know him," I said. "Oh, you know him?" and suddenly the kid is excited. And that led him to talk about his faith with his teacher, which makes him feel important and known by that teacher.

Cindy: When the parents come for open house I just tell them that there is no way I can teach their children about

American history without talking about these people and the foundations of the country and what they were thinking about. It's right in the text.

Interviewer: Does any event stand out in which you particularly wanted to say more than you did?

Cindy: Unfortunately, we've had a number of students die. Our principal asks for a moment of silence.

Eric: And at the end he will say, "Amen." I think potentially that could get us into trouble. What is the law about that?

Angelica: It is sad, isn't it, that we might disobey a law by saying "Amen."

Eric: I don't really think that's sad. I think that is respecting other people in the class. This moment of silence can be used in any way you want. You can pray, you can think about the next test, you can remember the person who died, but when someone says "Amen," it becomes a religious thing, and I'm not sure I think that's fair.

Suzanne: I have heard prayers offered at local ball games, school board meetings, school functions. I don't happen to agree with prayers over the intercom in a public school setting, but it seems in other parts of the country the pendulum has swung so wildly in the opposite direction. One's underlying philosophy and beliefs are bound to come out—*must* come out—if one is a person of integrity. If I had a child whose teacher was Buddhist or Mormon, I would certainly expect that over the course of the year my child would learn more about Buddhism or Mormonism. I would not have a problem if teachers were educating my child in these areas; I would have a problem if they were proselytizing.

Cindy: I think one nice option is that after hours you may say whatever you want, and if kids really want to know something, you can always invite them back after hours to talk. Then there isn't any issue concerning the fact that you are a public school teacher. I think kids long to be real. They want someone to whom they can say, "This is who I am." So I think there are different options. In English I teach "Sinners in the Hands of an Angry God" by Jonathan Edwards. The discussions that come out of that are amazing. We talk about the fact that some people say the world at one time was perfect and now it's this way. Recently, for the first time, I had a student say, "Well, you can't teach us this." I answered, "You know, if I were trying to convert you, you are right. But we're looking at a piece of literature, and if you think someone is going to be converted by Jonathan Edwards screaming at them, you can agree with me that that's not a good technique to use." We write "God" and "hell" on the chalkboard. I ask whether we talk that way today. We agree that today we talk mostly about God is love. We talk about why people always want to go the way they do. We have great discussions.

What difficulties or frustrations have you faced as a Christian teaching in a public school?

Monty: Staff and politics. Those are the killers. For me they were, anyway. The kids were great. Among the staff there were outright atheists who, as the kids said, "Would just as soon spit on the cross." That's really difficult to deal with.

Tom: And those are the ones who would come in and say, "Well, you're not supposed to do this."

Interviewer: But percentage wise there must have been quite a few Christian teachers in those schools.

Marvin: Well, of the fifty teachers that I knew well, there were probably five of us. Very few attended church at all. A lot of the teachers talked about what they did on the weekend and how drunk they got. At another school where I taught, at least 75 percent of the staff would have said they were Christians. The whole moral tone of the school was different and shaped by that. In that school, when Bible readings were canceled because they were no longer legal, the teachers had "devotionals" every day with the students. They might read from the Koran, or a moralistic poem, or a story with a moral to it, and two or three days a week the readings were from the Bible. The only time there was ever any flack was when one of the teachers selected the passage from the Bible that said wives must submit to their husbands. I was in the staff room when that came over the public address system. The women in the staff room were livid. It was a poor choice of reading on his part.

Interviewer: You talked about a frustration about not telling the whole message. Does that constant frustration lead to burnout at some point? Where you just feel you have to get out of there? How do you deal with that?

Eric: Not for me. My classes are sort of like this discussion. Especially in debate. Someone will say, "Hi, how are you doing?" and the other will say, "What do you mean by that?"

Greg: I agree. I don't see any time when I've been frustrated about that. I love to be out in the hallway between classes, and a lot of what I can do is spend time talking with students in the hall. You'd be surprised how much can be talked about during those five minutes. A kid once said to me, "Do you say hi to everyone?" I said that I do because I don't want anyone to go through the day without having someone acknowledge their presence. So many of our kids go through a day on the fringes. No one talks to them. And it is, for me, like the greeting of Christ. I don't say, "I greet you in the name of the Lord Jesus Christ," but I think about it that way. I know there are kids who don't even have a class on my floor who will come up every day just so I'll say hi to them. It has to do with using your time and with using your gifts.

Angelica: It shows that you value them. You must or you wouldn't be out in the hall. You'd have other things to do.

Cindy: I think for me it is just the opposite. If I didn't believe, I might be very burned out at this point. I've been at my school for eight years. It's when I get home and can rejuvenate that I can go back to a foundation where I can say, "Okay, I can do this." That gives me the desire to be there for the right reason. I also hope that if I get to the point where I don't really care any more, someone tells me to get out. For me being a Christian is what keeps me going in my job in the public school. That's what revitalizes me.

How has a Christian worldview affected what you choose to teach? How does it affect the curriculum?

Jack: For me, it's affected what I *don't* teach. As a science teacher, at some point in time when I first started I was basically told, "You *will* teach evolution." At one point they'll say, "We're only teaching this as theory," but the way it is presented in the books and the way I am expected to teach it is as fact. A number of years back I said that I would not teach it as a fact, and I would not teach it by itself.

Also, when we look at something really intricate in biology, I am not supposed to say that it's obvious that God created it that way, but kids will bring up their own questions, like, "That's so intricate. How is that possible?" And I'll say,

"Well, now, think about it. Do you think things like that can happen accidentally?" In science we're always teaching cause and effect, so without ever having to say a word, children can think on their own, "That didn't just happen." So in my case, I think it's the way I teach, and sometimes it is what I don't teach.

As a music teacher, I teach students that music is an expression of our feelings and our beliefs, and that it shows the culture in which it was produced. I'm very fortunate that in our county we have not been prevented from using any music with reference to God, or even any sacred music, or music of holidays. As long as we are "all-inclusive," we are pretty much allowed to use what we wish. I've been thankful that that's the case. But I suppose out of all the music teachers in the area I concentrate more on Thanksgiving and Christmas, and even the third stanza of the "Star-Spangled Banner," which is my favorite of the three, and show students these types of things more than some other teachers might.

Monty: In most situations I have been in, we were pretty free to talk about beliefs, but you have to be authentic. The kids will pick up on whether or not you are emotionally tied to what you are saying. They start asking questions when they see it is authentic.

Audrey: I find that students really are sensitive and do pick up what you believe. I remember teaching a poem in an eighth grade class, and one of the students said to me, "It sounds like a Christian poem the way you explain it. We had the same poem last year and it was entirely different then." They could sense from the way I questioned them.

Eric: Teaching about religion fits into world history class. And, of course, any literature class that alludes to it.

Greg: I'm reading Mark Twain now. In literature there are some things from the Bible you are expected to know.

Eric: Can the Bible be read as literature in a public school classroom? I went to the public school years ago and we used to memorize Psalm 23 and 1 Corinthians 13. A long time ago in the school in which I teach, we had a course in the classics, and the woman who taught it taught the Book of Job.

Suzanne: I am happy to have a free hand in choosing materials to use with my students. I try to use literature with them that will probe at life on a deeper level, literature that has such inescapably "religious" themes that it would be wrong *not* to teach it from such a perspective.

A favorite author is Oscar Wilde. He was quite a terrible role model, but he wrote some achingly lovely fables and fairy tales. I explain to the students what a parable is and ask them to think about what such a story might mean on another level. I often use Wilde's "The Nightingale and the Rose," a story of ultimate sacrifice and utter ingratitude. This leads naturally into a discussion of other ultimate sacrifices, and most of the time the students are the ones who bring up *the* sacrifice. Another of Wilde's stories, "The Selfish Giant," tells of a giant whose love for a child warmed and changed his heart. At the end of the tale the child returns with the print of nails on his hands and feet, which he says are "the wounds of Love."

Is it possible to have a Christian framework that helps you make decisions about how to act or how to plan curriculum? And is that something you can share with student teachers or inexperienced teachers who are Christians?

Greg: Well, I think it is contingent upon us to do that. The thing I told my student teacher this year was when you go into your first building find someone you can trust and can talk with. On the other hand, from my side as a veteran teacher, I try to seek out student teachers and new teachers and say, "My door's always open." But that isn't enough. You still have to keep going back and checking and after that there has to be a time for people to sit and talk. At our school a group of teachers tries to get together on Fridays. A lot of times we can draw in new people and they listen to us tell our war stories. It is reassuring to find out that others have the same kind of troubles and have learned to deal with them. I've found that to be very helpful. And often in the end, while it has helped the other person, it has helped me also.

Angelica: Do you mean a personal framework? Perhaps what new teachers need to hear from those of us who have taught longer is that we didn't create these problems, but in the meantime we will do what we can. You ought to have some idea that you are not going to remediate this problem once and for all. You do what you can and what you are not able to do is what haunts you day and night. You say, "Well, I need to act on my faith and when justice is needed I will intervene." But sometimes you encounter other Christians and they just don't help in the situation in the way you expect them to.

Interviewer: You mean that other Christians can be disappointing in their lack of involvement.

Greg: I'd say that sometimes is the biggest problem.

Angelica: You do what you need to do and you run up against the system.

Greg: Unfortunately, that's one of the reasons we lose good teachers in the urban areas. The system at times says,

"If I can get rid of you, I can get someone else easily. And probably that person won't complain as much."

Eric: Unfortunately, there is an attitude outside the city that often says, "We made it. My parents made it. Why can't those people in the city make it? I see a lot of racism and a lot of sexism in the name of Christianity in the speeches that the students give. This is their idea of Christianity and it is so sad.

Angelica: What do you do then? Do you address that?

Eric: I see my role as a speech teacher to ask questions, to play the devil's advocate without expressing my own opinion. Then kids, of course, will say, "We don't know what you think." I am opposed to what they're saying but I just ask the questions.

Angelica: That's the experience that the new teacher wouldn't have. Eric is saying exactly what he wants to say, but it's said so well that it is not offensive and they may not discover that they have just heard his opinion. That's the skill of the good teacher.

Eric: People will often say, "Why don't you ever take sides?" after we have talked about abortion or euthanasia. They'll say, "What do you think?" At some point I come right out and say it.

Greg: That's because the kids find you a person of value and they really care about your opinion.

Eric: And I try to say that my opinion doesn't mean anything more in this discussion than their opinions do. I worry that if I give my opinion too freely students who disagree will be afraid to talk.

Interviewer: The students are caught in the middle. On the one hand they respect their parents, and on the other hand they want to be liked by their peers. The teacher is the one who stands in the middle and the only one they may have the courage to talk to.

Greg: That answers the question why Christians are so needed in public schools.

Eric: I'd hate to have a situation in which Christian teachers only taught in Christian schools. I really believe that if you would take all Christian teachers out of the public schools it would be very sad.

Is there an emphasis on the teaching of morals or values in your school? If so, has there been discussion concerning what underlying principles might guide this instruction?

Suzanne: In terms of teaching morals, since life is inherently religious, everyone teaches from a moral perspective of some sort. Our school doesn't give any particular guidelines in this area, but we have had several antidrug speakers at school this year who have approached the issue from a religious and spiritual perspective. Interestingly, it seems that substance abuse is one thing everyone seems to agree is wrong. I don't understand why some people who insist on this are the very ones who consider something like premarital sex to be a matter of choice. When the opportunity presents itself, I try to be very clear with my students that it's not right to sleep with someone before committing to them in marriage. Apart from the Christian aspect of this, on a purely pragmatic level I have had too many pregnant teenagers and students with venereal disease, and I don't think we as teachers can afford to be prevaricating on moral issues. I feel duty bound to deal with racial issues every year, first because it is right that I do so, second because it means so much to my African American students, and third because I also teach a few racists who need to be forced out of their comfort zones! There are some short stories on film—Ernest J. Gaines's "The Sky Is Gray" and Richard Wright's "Almost a Man"—that are excellent in this area. Another thing that worked out this year was that the whole cloning issue came out in the news at the very time we were reading *Frankenstein,* so you can see that the whole discussion of who has the right to create life was very relevant.

Marilyn: The emphasis on teaching morals hasn't been discussed sufficiently in my school.

Ruth: I work on certain things such as not fighting, using decent language, being kind, not lying or cheating, and doing your best.

Joel: Yes. I haven't gotten into a discussion of underlying principles, though, because I don't know how to approach it.

Priscilla: I believe that morals and values are taught on a daily basis through our rules in the classroom, our actions as teachers, things we say and don't say, and ways that we deal with student problems. We haven't really discussed this as a group of teachers, however.

Andy: Right now our curriculum team is looking at these "pillars" and is trying to analyze how and where they are taught in each grade level's curriculum. I think this will be a big educational issue in the near future.

Marvin: In my school there is an emphasis on values, but it is not a direct part of the curriculum. Is there discussion of it? Not to my knowledge.

Glenda: As an elementary school teacher I get the opportunity to teach a lot of values that conform to Christianity. We have the opportunity to teach that every day.

Marvin: Education is the continuation of the values taught at home. You have the value taught at home that punctuality is not important and Dad complains about his boss being a terrible person so he as a worker won't do any more than he has to because the union will protect his rights. That's this generation, and it is being passed to the next.

Monty: You are dealing with the rights thing again, rights without responsibility.

Luke: Well, I think I've had to learn to get away from thinking of what's right and wrong and deal more with what is, and try to learn to accept these kids for what and where they are. Still, we try to instill some of what we believe. Some of them don't really see things to be wrong the way we see them to be right or wrong. To them it's normal. So we have to be really careful how we convey our beliefs to them in a nonjudgmental form. If we judge them too quickly, it's almost like we are being self-righteous.

Interviewer: But how do you answer them if they say, "Well, who says that that is wrong?" Their families haven't taught them what is wrong.

Luke: A question came up in my class last spring when an armored truck outside Detroit opened and a million dollars blew out the back. People were picking it up and turning it in. But one truck stopped and the driver drove off with $180,000. So the question was, "What would you do if you were in that truck?" The immediate response of my sixth graders was, "As soon as that money flew out of the truck it was free. I have no moral obligation." So how do we influence these kids? They believed it was perfectly free money even though they knew the money came from that truck. That's where my faith would tell me this money doesn't belong to me. It may be Christian or just simply moral, but the right thing to do would be to give the money back. But 85 percent of the kids in that class believed that if they were behind the armored truck, they would have kept the money. Because, after all, the truck drivers lost it.

Sarah: My students would have known the money should have gone back. Whether they would have given it back is a different question. I was thinking that we have reasons why we, as teachers, do things. One is that it is professional to respond to students one way or another in a given situation.

But it seems to me as a Christian that a more fundamental reason why I respond the way I do is because of how I should be responding as a Christian teacher. I must not be judgmental. If I see a child is doing something inappropriate, I shouldn't just assume she knows it is inappropriate. I should give the child the opportunity to answer for herself, explaining what was happening. Now she may feed me a line, which may or may not be true because kids are very adept at covering their tracks. However, I can find out eventually whether or not the child was telling the truth. But I shouldn't just blatantly judge. And it's easy to do that. It's easy to catch a student and nail them for doing something wrong without asking about the circumstance, what she was thinking. Often when you ask, you will find out it was quite different from what you thought. So I feel like I have a responsibility, as a Christian, to ask children to explain what they were doing so that I don't misjudge them and deal with them inappropriately.

In response to the question as to why something is wrong, I use the family analogy. I say to the students, "Your family has its own set of rules that you live by. Your family's rules might very well be different from someone else's. Classrooms are the same way. In my classroom this is not acceptable behavior. These are my classroom rules. In another situation that might be allowed, but not in my classroom." Maybe that is less definitive than saying it is wrong. It simply is not appropriate for this classroom.

Interviewer: You have different populations in your schools. Do your students always understand that a teacher has authority? That a teacher stands in the position of authority?

Jessica: Some do and some don't. I don't know if it is because they've never known authority. I think a lot of kids in our school have been their own caregivers, so they are home by themselves and don't have someone there in authority a lot of the time to tell them what is right or wrong. So when you as a teacher step in to tell them, they look at you and wonder, "Who are you to tell me what to do?"

Luke: We were studying Glasser's idea of "Quality Schools." The trend there is for teachers to be friends of students and not authority figures. The underlying premise is that kids will feel more comfortable seeing a teacher as a friend. Children will want to do better than if they see their teacher as an authority figure or a boss who lords it over them. We've tried this over the years, but it doesn't seem to work, at least it hasn't worked for me. As soon as I try to be their friend, they seem to think we are on the same level, and they try to manipulate or take advantage of me.

Interviewer: We don't work that way in a family, do we? Even with adolescents there still come points when, after all the discussion is over, if there is still disagreement then what the parent says goes. At least we hope it does.

Sarah: There is another component to it. In order to grow up to be an independent adult, they, in some respects, have to stand up against authority, to reason with it and to talk with it. If we act like their buddies, aren't we denying them something important? Don't they need that structure? Of course, we're talking about a good kind of authority, right? Not authority that is misused. I don't think I consciously try to be their friend, but I do try to be friendly with them so that I can carry on a conversation. I see my role with students as a nurturing, comforting role. That may be because I am a woman. No matter what happens to them, whether they have done something very terrible, the first thing I will do is put my arm around that student and say, "Well, it happened," so that they don't feel so alone.

Ruth: One of the things I recall saying to my students was, "It's very important that you listen to your mother and father. What they want you to believe is your first priority because you are their child."

Interviewer: Are the parents' values always similar to yours?

Jessica: Parents at my school have objected because children were taught that if someone fights with you, you must not fight back. These parents said that if their child doesn't fight back, he or she will be in trouble when they come home.

Ruth: You mean, if they get hurt at school because they didn't fight back, their parents will give them trouble because they didn't fight back?

Jessica: Yes, and they must stick up for a younger brother or sister.

Luke: Parents are trying to teach their children how to defend themselves on the street. And they are applying street rules to the school. We have to let them know that here we go by classroom rules. You have to disassociate yourself from street rules. You have to clarify that. In our school we are teaching students to become peace-keepers and avoid fights. The initiative is to get kids involved so that if one starts to get into a fight, others will step in to prevent the fight. It is based on reward and punishment and peer pressure. If a student gets into a fight, it costs the entire class a treat at the end of two weeks. There is also a program about conflict resolution. Unfortunately, we aren't teaching kids to treat each other kindly through our program. It is simply a violence prevention program. What matters is that they don't get into a fight. So we aren't really teaching integrity and honesty.

Ruth: Roger and David Johnson have a mediation program that works well. Students act as mediators between other students. The research shows that when a student starts to act as a mediator for others, his or her own behavior starts to change. For example, say that you were in a fight and another student mediates between the two fighters. That doesn't really change your behavior. But when you mediate between two other students, that's when your behavior changes. It is really effective. But the students must take ownership by becoming mediators in order for it to work.

Within your various school settings, is there much discussion concerning a teacher's freedom to express personal beliefs or philosophies?

Marvin: The last interpretation I heard was that if one student asks a question, you are to let it go. If more than one ask, you may answer.

Audrey: I didn't wait for them to ask, really. I just said what I believe.

Monty: Well, it depends on the principal who is in charge. I was always very careful not to preach. When you start preaching in a public system, you're in trouble. Then it gets back to the principal, and whether or not the principal agrees with you, the principal has to take a stand and say, "No you're not allowed to do that."

Glenda: I have a Christian principal, so she and I talk a lot, but in general, with the whole faculty, no.

Joel: Or in my case, about once or twice a year I'm reminded, "Hey, you're doing a really good job, but remember, you're not supposed to share your faith."

Glenda: That's neat, though, that you do it enough that they feel they have to remind you!

Joel: Well, I've never brought it up at the wrong time or in the wrong way, and at the same time they'll say, "You have such a positive influence on children," and I always say, "The positive influence, if I have one, is because of what I am and what I believe."

Interviewer: Have any of you felt frustrated because you wanted to say more than you felt you could within a classroom setting?

Joel: I think we all do. I get frustrated. I mean I really would like to be able to share my faith and be totally transparent all the time and that isn't possible. Yet at the same time I try to temper that, knowing that God puts us into any job. When I work for someone else I owe them eight hours of work; I don't owe them eight hours of me getting paid while I go around and witness. So it's frustrating, but I guess it could be that way with anything; we all would like to do more to have that witness.

Glenda: Every year in third grade I read The Chronicles of Narnia to my class. In one of the books, Aslan, the main character who represents Christ, says to the children, "You won't be coming back to Narnia, because you came here so that you could get to know me better in your own world." For a lot of the kids, it goes right over their heads. They never hear that sentence or they never think to question me about it. But there are always a few kids who will say, "Well, who is he talking about? Who is he?" and it's frustrating to me that I can't carry on that conversation. I feel like that's going over the line for me. So all I say is, "Well, you think about it. Who do you think it could be?" And then I'll tell them to come to me after school when they have ideas, or something like that. But it bothers me every year that I can't carry on that conversation with the entire class.

Nathan: I think when it comes to our witness, I don't recall who the quote was attributed to, but it's something like "Witness at all times; use words if necessary." You have a positive influence on kids, and in many cases your positive influence is not because of the words you say but because of the person you are. One of my frustrations is that I sometimes feel we can't witness with a lot of words in class. But you can witness as a person all the time. On the one hand, there is some frustration, but on the other hand, if we know what the rules are and we follow the rules, we are able to do much more than some people believe we can do. We may have supervisors who say, "You can't do this," and we can turn right around and say, "Yes, we can." We are within our legal rights to do those particular things.

Kind of an amusing incident happened last year. We had a troublesome student who came to Christ. He was a student of mine, and because he had been in such a great deal of trouble, he had been released from school for a certain period of time. When he came back, he was very verbal and very direct with his witness, to the point that he had students gathering around him. He was really making a major impact, particularly in the eighth grade, to the alarm of the administration. The amusing part was that the administration wasn't quite sure what to do, and so they told him to stop, but he didn't. He gained a lot of publicity, to the point that he was on regional television. He was interviewed on the radio and in the newspapers, and he was very clear about what was the driving force in his life, much to the dismay of the administration and non-Christians. But their hands were basically tied because he was within his legal rights.

Jack: The administration actually had to apologize to him, didn't they, because they had overstepped their bounds?

Nathan: They certainly did.

Jessica: I remember a student asking me in class last year if I believed in God. I answered that I did. She wanted me to go on and describe what I thought God was and what God's purpose was, and I was afraid to get into too much discussion about it for fear that I would overstep the bounds of what is allowed and what isn't.

Ruth: Did you know her background?

Jessica: Her grandmother is very religious, and this student talks about being saved. When that happens in class, it is uncomfortable.

Ruth: Although that is when you may answer, instead of just volunteering that information.

Interviewer: But how much may you say at that point?

Jessica: That's the problem. And if I talk about it and another student says, "Well, I don't," I don't know how far to go.

Ruth: I had a student in class say that she didn't believe in God, and we just talked openly about it. She had been raised in a country that didn't encourage Christianity. I didn't make a big deal of it because I didn't want to alienate her or make her feel bad.

Interviewer: Do you ever get questions about creation or about how things happened at the beginning?

Ruth: Questions I've had about that have been in private conversations. I just say that I believe God created the world. It is not important to me whether a person believes it was in seven days or millions of years. The important thing is that God did it.

Marta: We have Jewish students in our school, and we allow their parents to come in and explain Jewish holidays to our students. Yet, as Christians we are not as comfortable explaining what we believe.

Ruth: I was just with a group of people, many of whom are teachers and principals in public schools, and the question we were discussing was "How much may you speak about your faith?" One principal said, "We polled the students in the school, and an overwhelming number of students said they want to celebrate Christmas as a religious event. Why do we have to deny it? We should not have to. We celebrate the other holidays too, but we certainly celebrate Christmas now."

Jessica: I can remember when a directive came out stating that we had to call religious days "holidays," and we had to be careful of the songs we sang.

Luke: Those were for programs, weren't they? I think, though, that what happens in the classroom is more important than the odd program that the school gives.

Jessica: But we were also told that we had to be careful what we had up on our walls in our classrooms.

Marta: We have changed our terminology. We talk about the "holiday program."

Jessica: We used to have a Christmas program with a manger scene, but now we can't do that anymore. We must be careful which songs are sung for a holiday program.

Luke: That is if it is held in the school building. My understanding is that, by law, if we do a Christmas program, an Islamic program, a Jehovah's Witness program—if we recognize all the faiths present in our school, it is not a problem. We must not give more time to one faith than to any other.

Ruth: But there isn't time to give them equal time.

Luke: Well, you could have pieces of each one in a program, out of respect for different beliefs.

Ruth: You mean an eclectic program. But we should not have to deny what exists.

Luke: But what does exist, though?

Ruth: If I have a student who belongs to the Jehovah's Witnesses, that child should not have to deny their own religion. The same is true of Jews or Christians. So what I do is say, "At Christmas time Christians celebrate this. Not everybody in the world believes this way." I think it is important that they can acknowledge what they believe rather than deny it.

Luke: But the law is not about having them deny their faith. It is more a matter of how you mention it.

Marta: The principal at our school told us to take our classes to see the Christmas program at the local community center. It was the religious story of Christmas. He said that if any parents complained, he would tell them he had told us to do that.

Interviewer: Do you think he would say such a thing right now?

Luke: I think he would. I think as a Christian it is our responsibility to let the students know what we believe but to explain that it is perfectly fine if they believe differently. Tolerance is very much what being a Christian is about. In the past some Christian schools made sure students knew that Roman Catholics were wrong because they didn't have transubstantiation correct, and that other forms of Protestantism were wrong as well. We had blinders on in the eighth grade about what was right or wrong. I don't think that is appropriate.

Glenda: In the newspaper recently, didn't a principal suspend a kid because he brought a Bible for DEAR (Drop Everything And Read) time? The principal was wrong, and he was made aware that he was wrong, but he thought he was doing the right thing.

Ruth: I understand there is a law now that teachers may have a Bible on their desks.

Interviewer: I think that is for federal offices.

Luke: You may have Bibles in public schools, but then you must have a Koran or any other religious book as a form of literature.

Ruth: But if I am a Christian, I don't think I need to have the other religious books on my desk.

Luke: If you are using the Bible to share what it's about, you need to give the same kind of time to books of other belief systems. There has to be equal representation.

Eric: I keep a Bible on my desk all the time. The Gideons distributed them, and every once in a while someone will make a reference in a speech, and we want to check it in the Bible. Is that wrong in a public school?

Greg: Every day I do a saying for the day, and at times it is from the Bible. Sometimes it is just a pun, though. And kids have their Bibles there and look things up.

Angelica: Why would students have Bibles in school?

Greg: Oh, in any down time, they are very organized and they sit and read the Bible. It's amazing because I've got a lot of kids who can't even read that well.

Ruth: In teaching about religions, it might be good to point out things we have in common with Moslems, such as refraining from alcohol and attending night clubs. Those things have a negative impact on the culture. Maybe, when we think of different religions, we should think of what we have in common.

Do students at your school form clubs that are specifically for Christians?

Cindy: I run Fellowship for Christian Athletes in high school. At times I just post a notice on the board saying we're going to go somewhere together.

Interviewer: Do you meet after school?

Cindy: Before school. We may meet as long as it is on our own time. I don't have to be there until a quarter to the hour, so we meet before that. My kids run it. I am just there, but not as a leader. I just make sure it is organized. They run the Bible studies, bring in the guest speakers, and choose the videos. So it is student-run. The school newspaper said it is illegal, but I have documentation that I have given to the principals, and they are very good about it.

Interviewer: And you may post a sign about meetings?

Cindy: Yes. We also have Campus Crusade for Christ and Young Life, and they both advertise the same way. My group is more for kids who already are Christians and want to know more about the Bible. But their representatives meet with kids during lunch in the cafeteria.

Eric: A lot of kids question the legality of that.

Cindy: It is my understanding that there is no preaching at that time. But the school has been very open to that.

Eric: I've had some kids who have complained that the woman from the outside organization who meets with them in the cafeteria kind of badgers them. One of my students is a Mormon, and when the woman found that out, she apparently said, "You know, as a Mormon you cannot possibly be a Christian." I don't know about the legality of that.

Cindy: It's all going to come down to who presses the issue. If the issue is not pressed, it will go forward, but if a parent of that student had pressed it, I think it would have stopped.

Eric: I think it's out of place to actually judge someone as to whether or not they are Christian. I have a problem with that.

Joel: I think and I hope that people are becoming more educated. During my first year of teaching in the 1980s, because of the efforts of one student and one family who were nominally Jewish, the Fellowship of Christian Athletes was kicked out of school. After some Supreme Court rulings, it was reestablished last year. So some of those things are coming back, and I think that's good. The confrontations haven't really hit the high school where I teach now. As a matter of fact, there have been positive things such as prayer at the flagpole. When people see a bunch of kids standing around a flagpole, I think they are challenged in their own faith. "See, these kids don't mind doing that, and here I am hiding the fact that I'm a Christian." I think some people are challenged then to be a little more vocal about their faith.

Greg: I don't understand the reason for having these groups around the flagpole. I certainly consider myself a Christian, but I believe the commands in the Bible about being private about your prayer. God sees in private and rewards openly. I don't see the reason for flagpole prayers. Isn't there a danger in being like the Pharisees?

Cindy: There is a beauty, though, in people coming together for the purpose of prayer.

Glenda: Here's something that made me sad. This spring the students had clubs after school once a week for six or seven weeks. The leadership was strictly voluntary, and I wondered if my colleague Mary was going to do Good News Club because she had done so at another school. She said she was not allowed to do it, which really surprised me. She said a parent could come in and volunteer to do it, but she as a faculty member couldn't. That doesn't make sense to me, because it's voluntary and it's after school.

Maxine: But it is the law, because I had the same experience. We had some kids trying to begin a Bible club after school last year. I was the sponsoring teacher who stayed after school, but I wasn't allowed to participate in the prayer time. I wasn't allowed to help in the teaching of it at all. I wasn't allowed to write announcements. But it is true, because I looked it up in the Rutherford Institute guidelines. Because I'm an employee of the board of education, I am not allowed to actively participate. It has to be student-led or parent-initiated.

Nancy: Our school secretary, who is also a Christian, was interested in teaching that Good News Club, and Mary explained to her that she could not do it either because she is a school employee.

Have any of you been approached by Christian parents who have had concerns about curriculum and textbooks?

Joel: Yes, although when they found out I was a Christian, they said they had prayed for a Christian teacher. I've had a number of Christian children end up in my class. I think that's God's leading because then they aren't going to be made to feel inferior for believing in creation. Once Christian parents know who you are, they're your allies.

Priscilla: I had a parent who was concerned about a science unit dealing with the rain forest. This parent pointed out to me that I was talking mostly about saving the rain forest, rather than that man should have dominion over the trees and animals.

George: I have had parents concerned about the trade books dealing with witches and such at Halloween. I pull any questionable books out of my library.

Jack: I had an incident a couple of years ago with a parent who came in and confronted me because I had taught a song to first graders that made reference to an angel. It came out in the conversation that she was an atheist, and therefore, did not want her child exposed to any reference to religion at all. I was very thankful that I understood what my rights are. I was able to tell her that in the public school, reference can be made to anything in our society, including religion. I told her that I was very much within my rights and within the curriculum.

Andy: The only content area that has raised concern is the Michigan Health Model. It has been thrown out in the past, but it has been revised and accepted by the board. I still use my own judgment in areas I don't feel comfortable with and offer parents a chance to view any materials I use.

Marilyn: The concern at my school has been more with holiday parties than textbooks. We have changed the name of parties to "fall fun" (Halloween), "winter holidays" (Christmas), and "friendship" (Valentine's Day). One year we tried to omit costumes or try storybook costumes for Halloween, but many parents protested, so now we dress in costumes. However, many children do not come that day because their parents are opposed.

Laura: One parent objected to our teaching about African Americans and Martin Luther King, in particular. He said we need to teach only about Lincoln and Washington and not about King. I showed him how our curriculum is put together so that we also teach white history.

Matthew: Parents in my school do exempt their children from certain learning units such as reproductive health. They are allowed to do that by law.

Whenever I have non-Christian students, I ask them to be a resource for their religion. They share their beliefs, and we compare their culture, including religion, with other American cultures, including religion. For example, I explain that the reason the United States has so many different religions is because long ago some Christian leaders believed God did not want people to suffer at the hands of others because of their belief or nonbelief in God. I tell them about Roger Williams and others.

Marilyn: One time I had a mother tell me that they began sending their child to Sunday school because she was asking questions resulting from things I had mentioned about God's creation. Then they decided they would go to church with their daughter. She thanked me for leading them to Christ in a rather indirect way.

Jack: I've had Christian parents come to my classroom on a conference day and ask me if I was a Christian.

Glenda: Because of what you taught?

Jack: Just simply because of what their children went home and said. I just praise the Lord that even though I feel so inhibited, sometimes something is coming across. It's the Holy Spirit.

Nancy: We had an incident in our school a couple of years ago with a parent who was concerned about a book that was in our media center. Our principal is a Christian, and she was very willing to listen to what the parent had to say. When the principal reviewed the book, she felt very strongly that it should be pulled. Since then, I believe the book has been removed from all the media centers in the county.

Maxine: If parents want to preview the health and family living curriculum, including sex education, and they can't come to the meeting, they come to me to see it. I really appreciate the opportunity to do that because what I want to do is encourage those parents as much as I can to keep on top of what's going on in the schools. And so I say, "You all are wise to come here and not just assume that what's being taught is acceptable. I commend you for taking the time." In that way I feel like I do encourage Christian parents to stay involved in what's going on.

Which religions are taught about in your school, and what qualifications are expected of the teacher who teaches about them?

Joel: I've been told by one of the teachers that they only teach the "major" religions: Hinduism, Buddhism, Islam, Judaism, and Christianity. Unfortunately, the qualifications of the teachers are not very good. On a student trip, I had a chance to look through the notes of students who were studying for a religion test. The teachers have tried to be objective. But they didn't have any part of Christianity right. As a matter of fact, they were more accurate on the other religions than they were on Christianity. They taught Christianity as a good works, follow the ten commandments kind of thing. I guess that doesn't bother me that much because most of the kids know better anyway, but it just seems really odd that in America the one religion they can't get right in class is Christianity.

I know one teacher has told a number of his classes that to him the religion that makes the most sense—and right there he's stepped over the boundary—is Buddhism. And this is what he's entitled to? I know students who are devout Christians who would contradict something he said, and he would say, "Well now, I'm teaching this and I know what's going on." At least the students are vocal. We had a course in Bible as literature that isn't being taught now.

Jack: Why is that?

Joel: Lack of interest or the direction the curriculum is going now.

Tom: At one point, we had a course in Old and New Testament for students who wanted to major in English literature. They needed that background to understand the allusions found in English literature. The teacher had a religious background but wasn't absolutely certain he was a believer.

Monty: In the last ten years I have noticed such a decrease in my students' understanding and ability to talk about spiritual matters. If I talk about spiritual life, it's almost as if they don't know what I'm talking about.

Tom: In some staff rooms there is a movement toward New Age thinking. Many teachers are interested in a book called the *Celestine Prophecies*. That is spirituality without morality and without a deity. It is probably quite rife in the schools now I would think.

Do you feel you have received support from people in your church about your calling to teach in a public school?

Nancy: I think one way our church supports us is its view that we are called to this ministry in the public school. For some people the call is to teach in a Christian school, and for others the call is to teach in a public setting. I think that we feel a lot of support for the fact that we're called to this particular ministry.

Tom: Well, I think in some communities people are not quite certain you are as Christian as those who teach in Christian schools.

Priscilla: Yes, I get support from Christian friends just by talking to them about stressful weeks or days. I also discuss what I can do about certain students and they pray for them.

Marie: I feel I am supported more because I teach special education rather than simply teaching in a public school. I do struggle with this aspect, especially when it comes to Sundays when my church emphasizes Christian education and the importance of sending children to Christian schools. What about those families who cannot afford it or simply choose not to send their kids to a Christian school?

Matthew: I have heard many people say, "Thank you for being a Christian teacher." They feel more comfortable knowing that I am a Christian. I know they pray for me. We pray together. Christian school teachers, public school teachers, home school teachers all pray together for each other.

A teachers' support group would be helpful. Christian teachers in a building should support each other, especially when under attack.

Dorothy: I know of a church that makes the public school part of its servant work. A group of people are committed to helping out in the school, tutoring the children.

Joel: I feel a lot of prayer support for Christian teachers. For me, that's the best kind.

Angelica: It seems, though, that among some Christians, there still is some feeling against our being in the pubic school.

Do you ever feel a sense of isolation, a feeling of aloneness as a Christian teaching in a public school? It is often felt especially by those who believe their faith must be part of all that they do.

Audrey: One of the things I learned from Tom was the tremendous importance of prayer in our work as public school teachers. I would like to teach teachers about the importance of prayer. I recently met a young teacher who was dreading going back to school in September. She said, "I find it so difficult. I didn't anticipate this at all. I don't know what to expect of my principal and my fellow teachers because there has been a change. And I have so many difficult students in my class." I said to her, "How much time do you spend in prayer?" She looked at me and said, "What do you mean?" I said, "Have you ever considered going to school early in the morning and then praying at the desk of each student before they arrive? And praying for your principal? And praying for your fellow staff members?" It really works.

Tom: I believe that you claim that classroom as holy ground. In the name of Jesus you claim that classroom.

There is a spiritual reality. We are commanded to put on spiritual armor. Sometimes the light is so dim. We have a generation raised without Scripture, raised on what is good for you.

Charles: My church has been very supportive. A number of church members have come to talk to me about what it is like to be a Christian teaching in a public school. They are very sensitive and respectful and think we have tough jobs. We have, in the past, had support groups of Christian and public school teachers in our church.

In my home community, my parents informed the principal and others that I now teach in a public school. There were people who frowned on that. It is almost as if they feel if you don't get a job teaching in a Christian school you should not teach. You should go into another area of work entirely.

Interviewer: What can we say to college students who are preparing to teach concerning teaching in public schools. Some have come all the way through Christian schools, and they don't dare to teach anywhere else because they have heard horror stories. Others believe that teaching in a public school can be as much a person's calling as any other job in life.

Ruth: One reason I didn't get any flack about teaching in a public school was because I made it clear that I truly believed God was calling me there. Perhaps tell them that there are many graduates of our college who teach in public schools, and they really feel good about their opportunity to teach there. Simply tell them that people are people. They have the same needs, the same desire to be loved. Whether you are talking about staff people or about students in a public school, they are people and are God's children.

Interviewer: Someone in an interview said that when she first taught in a public school, she kept herself isolated from other teachers because she couldn't see that they were Christians.

Ruth: My first experience of teaching was in a public school, and I was amazed how much I had in common with teachers from other faith groups, such as Roman Catholicism. One Catholic woman, in particular, was a devoted Christian, as was I. We had so much in common.

Charles: My first teaching experience was in a public school, and one day the principal, a Christian, asked, "Charles, if Jesus were to come back to earth today, what school do you think he would teach in, a Christian school or a public school? I had to sit back and think about that. Would he go to a school where the kids were already Christians?

Ruth: I have a sister who prays for any student I ask her to pray for. Maybe you should say to your college students, "Those of you who choose to teach in a public school must remember that you have the whole body of Christ to help you by praying for you and your students. Find a person you respect in your church and ask that person to pray for you. Tell that person the specific needs of the students in your classroom. You are not without support just because you may not have around you a large body of Christian teachers."

Charles: It never entered my mind that if I became a public school teacher I would make more money than in a Christian school, and yet that is the perception of some people. You don't go into teaching at all if you are thinking about making a lot of money.

Marta: A problem I continue to struggle with is teaching in a public school and sending my children to a Christian school. On the staff it has been questioned. I feel sort of defensive that they might think it is an attitude that this school isn't good enough for my children. People don't easily accept that we send them to a Christian school out of conviction.

Ruth: You know what they don't understand? The fact that in a Christian school your faith is being integrated into every topic, the entire day, in everything the teacher does. People don't realize that. They think that going to a Christian school means you pray and study the Bible. They don't understand integration.

Jessica: It's interesting that you said that because I have thought the same thing about people who send their own children to the Christian school while they teach in the public school. But once it was explained to me I understood. When I first thought about it, I thought it was a way for their children to be isolated from a certain group of people.

Marta: In the interview with our new public school superintendent, she was asked about the 35 to 40 percent of children in this city who go to private or parochial schools, and she said, "I know there are some people who do that to escape the public school, but many people do it out of conviction, and this makes for a rich community."

Ruth: What I miss the most about not teaching in a Christian school is the prayer time. When the children told me what they wanted us to pray for, I knew where every child was coming from. I knew whose grandmother was dying and whose father was out of town. I really miss that opportunity to know the needs of the children.

If you are a Christian teaching in a public school, there surely will be times when you feel lonely and overwhelmed by the task confronting you. There will be days when you sense that the school and your classroom, a place that exists for the common good, is cracking into pieces, and you fear that it or you may shatter completely. Let the words of these teachers remind you that you are not alone in living out your calling. Know that you are surrounded by a great cloud of witnesses, teachers who believe what you believe and who struggle as you struggle.

Teachers like these are all around us, serving in our nation's schools. By faith they live their calling, knowing that the day is coming when all people will recognize Jesus Christ as Lord. Until that time, while we wait, we are grateful for their lives and their witness.

Appendix A

Resources

American Association of School Administrators
Andrew Rotherham
1801 N. Moore Street
Arlington, VA 22209
703-528-0700
Fax: 703-528-2146
This organization can answer questions regarding religious expression in public schools.

American Center for Law and Justice
Jay Alan Sekulow, Chief Counsel
P.O. Box 64429
Virginia Beach, VA 23467
757-579-2489
Web site: http://www.aclj.org
Contact: Colby May
Office of Government Affairs
1000 Thomas Jefferson Street N.W.
Washington, DC 20007
202-337-2273
The ACLJ is a nonprofit public interest law firm and educational organization dedicated to the promotion of pro-liberty, pro-

life, and pro-family causes. The center engages in litigation, provides legal services, renders advice and counsel to clients, and supports attorneys who are involved in defending the religious and civil liberties of Americans.

A Parent's Guide to Religion in the Public Schools
The National Congress of Parents and Teachers
Web site: http://www.fac.org/publicat/parents/parents.htm

California 3 Rs Project: Putting Haynes's 3Rs into Practice
777 Camino Pescadero
Isla Vista, CA 93117
805-961-9335

Catholic League for Religious and Civil Rights
William A. Donohue, President
1011 First Avenue
New York, NY 10022
703-538-5085
Contact: Kenneth Whitehead
Board of Directors
The Catholic League defends the rights of Catholics—laypeople and clergy—to participate in American public life without defamation or discrimination.

Character Education Partnership
809 Franklin Street
Alexandria, VA 22314
800-988-8081
This organization is committed to developing civic virtue and moral character in our youth to create a more compassionate and responsible society.

Christian Educators Association International (CEAI)
Forrest Turpen, Executive Director
P.O. Box 41300
Pasadena, CA 91114
626-798-1124
Fax: 626-798-2346
E-mail: ceaieduca@aol.com

Temporary web site: http://members.aol.com/ceaieduca/CEAI/
ceaihome.htm.
This is an association of seven thousand Christians who teach
in public schools. The Association believes in and supports public schools. Conferences are provided along with an Internet di-
rectory of members.

Christian Legal Society
  Sam Casey, Executive Director
  4208 Evergreen Lane
  Suite 222
  Annadale, VA 22003
  703-642-1070
  Web site: http://www.cls.com
  Contact: Steve McFarland, Director of Center for Law and Re-
    ligious Freedom
The legal advocacy arm of the Christian Legal Society is the
Center for Law and Religious Freedom. It comprises a network of
volunteer attorneys defending religious freedom in their com-
munities, in the high courts, and in Congress.

*Diversity and Faithfulness: Reflections for Christian Teachers on Plural-
ity and Pluralism in Canadian Public Schools*
  Task Force on Education
  The Evangelical Fellowship of Canada, M.I.P.
  Box 3745
  Markham, ON L3R 0Y4

Freedom Forum
  Charles Haynes
  1101 Wilson Boulevard
  Arlington, VA 22209
  703-528-0800
  Fax: 703-284-2879
  E-mail: chaines@freedomforum.org
  Web site: http://www.freedomforum.org
This organization will answer questions concerning religious
expression in public schools. The web site lists frequently asked
questions and their answers.

National Council of Churches
Joan B. Campbell, General Secretary
475 Riverside Drive
New York, NY 10115
212-870-2227
Contact: Oliver Thomas, Counsel
1111 Melvin Avenue
Maryville, TN 37801
423-457-6466
This organization is a community of thirty-three member church bodies, including Protestant and Orthodox churches, which are related to more than 141,000 congregations across the country. The council has long maintained programs dealing with religious and social issues including civil rights, domestic social justice, worldwide relief and development, Christian education and Bible translation, and many other areas.

National Association of Evangelicals
Dr. Don Argue, President
1023 15th Street N.W.
Suite 500
Washington, DC 20005
202-789-1011
E-mail: oga@nae.net
Web site: http://www.nae.net
Contact: Forest Montgomery, Counsel
The mission of this organization is to extend the kingdom of God through a fellowship of member denominations, churches, organizations, and individuals; demonstrating the unity of the body of Christ by standing for biblical truth; speaking with a representative voice; and serving the evangelical community through united action, cooperative ministry, and strategic planning. This organization will answer questions regarding religious expression in public schools.

National School Boards Association
Laurie Westley
1680 Duke Street
Alexandria, VA 22314

703-838-6703
Fax: 703-548-5613
E-mail: lwestley@nsba.org
Web site: http://www.nsba.org
This organization will answer questions regarding religious expression in public schools.

Religion and Public Education Resource Center—Curriculum
California State University-Chica
Chica, CA 95929-0740
This center seeks to foster a greater understanding of the distinction between school-sponsored practice of religion and the academic study of religion.

U.S. Department of Education
Web site: http://www.ed.gov
http://www.ed.gov/speeches/08–1995/religion.html

Appendix B

Unit: The Wonder of Our World
Implementation Plan and Sequence of Lesson Plans

Chris Hondorp

Day 1: Michigan Wildflowers

art media: drawing and watercolor
art concepts: study of lines and shapes

Objectives

1. Students will examine and be exposed to several kinds of Michigan wildflowers through resources in the art room. We will look at real wildflowers up close and notice details in the creation of these flowers. We will discuss which flowers are on the endangered species list.
2. Students will come to know the Endangered Species Act of 1974 and learn how to protect our wildflowers.

Learning Activities

1. Students will make a list of their favorite wildflowers in their journals.
2. Students will draw some of their favorite wildflowers.
3. Students will add color to their drawings using various color schemes with watercolors.

Resources

Legend of Indian Paintbrush by Tommie de Paola
Michigan Wildflowers by Harry C. Lund
posters from the art room
real wildflowers brought in from the area (flowers *not* on the
endangered species list)

Day 2: Georgia O'Keefe Flowers

art media: drawing and tempera paint
art concepts: study of abstract vs. real

Objectives

1. Students will examine the works of Georgia O'Keefe, specifically her large flower details.
2. Students will learn why Georgia O'Keefe painted flowers so large.

Learning Activities

1. Students will make a list in their journals of the different flowers painted by Georgia O'Keefe.
2. Students will list five facts about Georgia O'Keefe.
3. Students will draw the details of some flowers on large white pieces of paper.
4. Students will paint their drawings with tempera paint.

Resources

prints of flowers by Georgia O'Keefe from the artwork reproductions collection in the art room
American Women: From Early Indian Times to the Present by Charlotte Rubenstein

Day 3: Bugs and Insects

art media: drawing with colored pencils, craypas, markers
art concept: study of design and pattern

Objectives

1. Students will study bugs and insects up close and look at the details of their bodies using a magnifying box.
2. Students will recreate the patterns on bugs and design their own bugs.

Learning Activity

1. Students will draw and color enlarged pictures of bugs and insects found in the Reading Rainbows book *BUGS*.

Resource

the book *BUGS*

Day 4: Garden Radial Design (part 1, summer scene)

art media: drawing with colored pencils, craypas, markers
art concept: radial design

Objectives

1. Students will review concepts and ideas they learned through the study of nature from journal entries.
2. Students will design their own summer view of a garden.

Learning Activities

1. Students will take a large white piece of paper and make a large circle with a small circle in the middle. Students will place a photograph of themselves in the center.
2. Students will divide the large circle into four segments, then design their own summer garden scene, drawing some of the flowers and bugs and insects they learned about.

Resource

Students will use their journal entries to design their garden view.

Day 5: Shapes of Trees

art media: sketches and photography
art concept: form, shape, and structure

Objectives

1. Students will understand that the artist makes shapes and sketches before adding details in drawings.
2. Students will appreciate that trees have geometric shapes.
3. Students will practice using a camera.

Learning Activities

1. Students will photograph different trees in their neighborhood when the fall color change is occurring.
2. Students will sketch main geometric shapes first, then turn those shapes into different shapes of trees.
3. Students will use their photos to determine different shapes of trees.
4. In their journals students will make a list of different kinds of trees.

Resource

Using money from PTA funds, I will buy disposable cameras for students to take home and photograph pictures of trees. I will need approximately two hundred dollars for this project.

Day 6: Leaf Collage

art media: paper cutouts; drawing with colored pencils, craypas, markers
art concepts: balance and rhythm

Objectives

1. Students will learn about Henri Matisse and his pattern designs.
2. Students will learn about symmetrical design and balance.

Learning Activities

1. Students will list five facts about Henri Matisse.
2. Students will draw pattern designs in the style of Henri Matisse.

Resources

art reproductions from the collection in the art room
Matisse by Lawrence Gowing
Henri Matisse by the UCLA Art Council

Day 7: Clay Stamps/Printing

art media: clay and tempera paint
art concept: patterns and design

Objectives

1. Students will design simple leaf stamps using clay.
2. Students will experiment with repeated patterns.

Learning Activities

1. Students will create some simple leaf stamps from clay, using simple leaf patterns.
2. Students will then print with their stamps, using the fall colors of leaves.
3. Students will create a repeated pattern design on their fabric.

Resources

fabric pieces cut into banner size
samples of former students' artwork

Day 8: Garden Radial Design (part 2, fall scene)

art media: drawing with colored pencils, craypas, markers
art concept: radial design

We will repeat steps and process from day 4 using a fall view of students' gardens.

Day 9: Winter Nature Scene

art media: sketches and photography
art concept: form, shape, and structure

We will repeat steps and process from day 5 using scenes of trees and gardens in winter.

Day 10: Clay Tiles

art medium: clay
art concept: slab construction of clay

Objectives

1. Students will be able to create clay tiles using slab formation concepts.
2. Students will be able to measure and cut tiles.

Learning Activity

1. Students will measure, cut, and design clay tiles for their gardens using clay tools and macaroni alphabets.

Resources

clay tools found in the art room
alphabet macaroni purchased from the grocery store

Day 11: Garden Sculpture

art medium: metal pieces
art concept: building three-dimensional objects using metal

Objectives

1. Students will examine various outdoor pieces of sculpture.
2. Students will look at the works of Alexander Calder.

Learning Activities

1. Students will design their own outdoor sculptures using pieces of metal.
2. Students will list and sketch various outdoor sculpture pieces we examined in class.
3. Students will sketch a few of their favorite outdoor sculptures in their journals.

Resource

Book of the Artists by Henry T. Tuckerman

Day 12: Garden Radial Design (part 3, winter scene)

art media: drawing with colored pencils, craypas, markers
art concept: radial design

We will repeat the process from day 4 using a winter view of students' gardens.

Day 13: Monet's Garden

art medium: clay
art concept: slab construction of clay

Objective

1. Students will examine the ponds in Claude Monet's garden through the study of his art reproductions in the art room, through the video *Linnea in Monet's Garden,* and through the book with the same title.

Learning Activities

1. Students will look at samples of waterlilies in the art room, studying the sizes and shapes, and then create their own waterlilies out of clay slabs.
2. Students will list different kinds of flowers found in Claude Monet's garden.

Resources

book and video entitled *Linnea in Monet's Garden*

Day 14: Landscape Architecture

art medium: papier-mâché

art concept: landscape as an art form with a history in other cultures

Objectives

1. Students will look at garden design using asymmetrical and symmetrical design as well as formal and informal design.
2. Students will see a sample of topiary.

Learning Activities

1. Students will look at various examples of the styles of garden stated in the objectives.
2. Students will create a topiary sculpture using papier-mâché.
3. Students will list different kinds of gardens and examples of each from notes taken during slide presentation.

Resource

slides in the art room showing samples of landscape architecture, specifically for the garden

Day 15: Tulip Time

art media: batik on fabric
art concept: color schemes used by Vincent van Gogh

Objectives

1. Students will examine the works of Vincent van Gogh.
2. Students will work with the color schemes used by Vincent van Gogh.
3. Students will discuss and examine different springtime flowers.

Learning Activities

1. Students will learn the art of batiking on fabric using a simple tulip design and using the color schemes of Vincent van Gogh.
2. Students will make a list of their favorite springtime flowers in their journals.

Resources

art books and art reproductions from the art room
samples of former students' batiking banners
muslin from fabric store

Day 16: Garden Radial Design (part 4, spring scene)

art media: drawing with colored pencils, craypas, markers
art concept: radial design

We will repeat steps and process from day 4 using a spring view of students' gardens.

Instruction in this unit will follow the Stronks and Blomberg (1993) model of immersion, withdrawal, and return. There will be four lessons in September, four in late fall, four in the winter, and four in the spring, with a final project at the end of the school year.

Reference List

Baer, Richard. (1987). In R. Neuhaus (Ed.), *Democracy and the renewal of public education* (pp. 1–27). Grand Rapids, MI: Eerdmans.

Bates, S. (1996). In C. Haynes & O. Thomas, *Finding common ground: A first amendment guide to religion and public education* (pp. 5.7–5.8). The Freedom Forum First Amendment Center, 1207 18th Avenue South, Nashville, TN 37212.

Cassity, M., Guinness, O., Haynes, C., Seel, J., Smith, T., & Thomas, O. (1990). *Living with our deepest differences: Religious liberty in a pluralistic society* (upper elementary edition). First Liberty Institute, Learning Connections Publishers, 75 Mt. Vernon Street, Boston, MA 02108.

Cooling, T. (1994). *A Christian vision for state education.* London: Society for Promoting Christian Knowledge.

Davis v. Beason, 133 U.S. 333 (1890).

Dillard, A. (1982). *Teaching a stone to talk.* New York: Harper & Row.

Edwards v. Aguillard, 482 U.S. 578 (1987).

Epperson v. Arkansas, 393 U.S. 97 (1968).

Equal Access Act, 20 U.S.C. 4071-74 (1984).

Faber, R. (1998). Personal communication.

Fowler, J. (1992). Character, conscience, and the education of the public. In F. Power & D. Lapsley (Eds.), *The challenge of pluralism: Education, politics, and values* (pp. 225–250). London: University of Notre Dame Press.

Glenn, C. (1988). *The myth of the common school.* Amherst: University of Massachusetts Press.

Glenn, C., & Glenn, J. (1992). Making room for religious conviction in democracy's schools. In S. Hauerwas & J. Westerhof (Eds.), *Schooling Christians* (pp. 88–114). Grand Rapids, MI: Eerdmans.

Grene, M. (1968). *Approaches to a philosophical biology.* New York: Basic Books.

Hartnett, S. E. (1997). What to do about students with chronic attendance problems. In H. Van Brummelen and D. Elliott (Eds.), *Nurturing Christians as reflective educators* (pp. 253–255). Azusa, CA: Coalition of Christian Teacher-Educators.

Hasseler, S. (1998) Personal communication.

Haynes, C., & Thomas, O. (1996). *Finding common ground: A first amendment guide to religion and public education.* The Freedom Forum First Amendment Center, 1207 18th Avenue South, Nashville, TN 37212.

Hill, B. (1982). *Faith at the blackboard.* Grand Rapids, MI: Eerdmans.

Hirsch, E. D. (1992). *What your fourth grader needs to know.* New York: Doubleday.

Holtrop S. (1997). Teaching Christianly: A responsibility model. In H. Van Brummelen and D. Elliott (Eds.), *Nurturing Christians as reflective educators* (pp. 51–65). Azusa, CA: Coalition of Christian Teacher-Educators.

Hondorp, C. (1998). Personal communication.

Huisman, S. (1998). Personal communication.

Ingber, S. (1989). Religion or ideology: A needed clarification of the religion clauses. *Stanford Law Review 41,* 233.

Jadrich, J. (1998). Personal communication.

Jaffree v. Board of School Comm'rs., 554 F.Supp. 1104 (S.D. Ala. 1983), aff'd in part, rev'sd in part, *Jaffree v. Wallace,* 705 F.2d 1526 (11th Cir. 1983), cert. denied sub nom. *Board of School Comm'rs v. Jaffree,* 466 U.S. 926 (1984); *Jaffree v. James,* 554 F.Supp. 1130 (1983), aff'd in part, rev'd in part sub nom. *Jaffree v. Wallace,* 705 F.2d 1526 (11th Cir. 1983), aff'd, 472 U.S. 38 (1985).

Johnson, P. (1993). *Darwin on trial.* Downers Grove, IL: InterVarsity Press.

Joldersma, C. (1997). Personal correspondence.

Kreeft, P. (1992). *Back to virtue: Traditional wisdom for modern moral confusion.* San Francisco: Ignatius Press.

Lantinga, S. (1998). Personal correspondence.

Lemon v. Kurtzman, 403 U.S. 602 (1971).

Marsden, G. (1997). *The outrageous idea of Christian scholarship.* New York: Oxford University Press.

Marzano, R. (1994). When two world views collide. *Educational Leadership 51* (4), 6–11.

Molnar, A. (1994). Fundamental differences? *Educational Leadership 51* (4), 4–5.

Mozert v. Hawkins County Public Schools, 579 F.Supp. 1051 (E.D. Tenn. 1984), 582 F.Supp. 201 (1984), reversed and remanded 765 F.2d (6th Cir. 1985).

Norris, K. (1996). *The cloister walk.* New York: Riverhead Books.

Palmer, P. (1990). "All the way down": A spirituality of public life. In P. Palmer, B. G. Wheeler, & J. W. Fowler (Eds.), *Caring for the commonweal: Education for religious and public life* (pp. 147–163). Macon, GA: Mercer University Press.

Piediscalzi, N., Will, P., & Swyhart, B. (1981). *Public education religion studies: An overview.* Missoula, MT: Scholars Press for the American Academy of Religion.

Religion, Education and U.S. Constitution. National School Board Association Council of School Attorneys. March 1994, Alexandria, Virginia.

Religion in the Public Schools: A Joint Statement of Current Law (April 1995). This is a joint statement by various organizations. The drafting committee includes the American Jewish Congress, American Civil Liberties Union, American Jewish Committee, American Muslim Council, Anti-Defamation League, Baptist Joint Committee, Christian Legal Society, General Conference of Seventh-day Adventists, National Association of Evangelicals, National Council of Churches, People for the American Way, Union of American Hebrew Congregations. Endorsing organizations include American Ethical Union, American Humanist Association, Americans for Religious Liberty, Americans United for Separation of Church and State, B'nai B'rith International, Christian Science Church, Church of the Brethren (Washington Office), Church of Scientology International, Evangelical Lutheran Church in America, Federation of Reconstructionist Congregations and Havurot, Friends Committee on National Legislation, Guru Gobind Singh Foundation, Hadassah (the Women's Zionist Organization of America), Interfaith Alliance, Interfaith Impact for Justice and Peace, National Council of Jewish Women, National Jewish Community Relations Advisory Council, National Ministries of the American Baptist Churches (USA), National Sikh Center, North American Council for Muslim Women, Presbyterian Church (USA), Reorganized Church of Jesus Christ of Latter Day Saints, Unitarian Universalist Association of Congregations, and United Church of Christ.

Religious Freedom Restoration Act, Pub. L. No. 103–141, 107 Stat. 1488 (1993).

Riley, R. Letter to public school superintendents. United States Department of Education, Washington, DC, 10 August 1995.

Schwartz, J. E. (1997). Christians teaching in public schools: What are some options? *Christian Scholar's Review 26* (3), 293–305.

Smith v. Board of School Comm'rs of Mobile County, 655 F.Supp. 939 (S.D. Ala. 1987), reversed 827 F.2d 684 (11th Cir. 1987).

Stronks, G. G., & Blomberg, D. (1993). *A vision with a task: Christian schooling for responsive discipleship.* Grand Rapids, MI: Baker Book House.

Trotter, D. (1998). Personal communication.

United States v. Seeger, 380 U.S. 163 (1965).

Van Manen, M. (1991). *The tact of teaching.* Albany, NY: State University of New York Press.

Whitehead, J. (1994). *The rights of religious persons in public education.* Wheaton, IL: Crossway Books.

The Williamsburg charter (1990). Washington, DC: The Brookings Institution.

Wolterstorff, N., & Audi, R. (1997). *Religion in the public square.* Lanham, MD: Rowman & Littlefield, Publishers.

Wright v. Houston Independent School District, 366 F. Supp. 1208 (S.D. Texas 1972), aff'd 486 F.2d 137 (5th Cir. 1973), cert. denied 417 U.S. 969 (1974).

Zylstra, B. (1991). The United States Constitution and the rights of religion. In R. McCarthy & J. Skillen (Eds.), *Political order and the plural structure of society* (pp. 315–332). Atlanta: Scholars Press.

Julia K. Stronks is a practicing attorney and associate professor of political and international studies at Whitworth College. **Gloria Goris Stronks** is professor of education at Calvin College and the (co)author/editor of four books, including *A Vision with a Task* (Baker, 1993).